Artificial Intelligence for Humans, Volume 1: Fundamental Algorithms

Jeff Heaton

Heaton Research, Inc.
St. Louis, MO, USA

Publisher: Heaton Research, Inc.
Artificial Intelligence for Humans, Volume 1: Fundamental Algorithms
December, 2013
Author: Jeff Heaton
Editor: WordsRU.com
ISBN: 978-1493682225
Edition: 1.1

purpose, or any losses or damages of any kind caused or alleged to be caused directly or indirectly from this book.

SOFTWARE LICENSE AGREEMENT: TERMS AND CONDITIONS

The media and/or any online materials accompanying this book that are available now or in the future contain programs and/or text files (the "Software") to be used in connection with the book. Heaton Research, Inc. hereby grants to you a license to use and distribute software programs that make use of the compiled binary form of this book's source code. You may not redistribute the source code contained in this book, without the written permission of Heaton Research, Inc. Your purchase, acceptance, or use of the Software will constitute your acceptance of such terms.

The Software compilation is the property of Heaton Research, Inc. unless otherwise indicated and is protected by copyright to Heaton Research, Inc. or other copyright owner(s) as indicated in the media files (the "Owner(s)"). You are hereby granted a license to use and distribute the Software for your personal, noncommercial use only. You may not reproduce, sell, distribute, publish, circulate, or commercially exploit the Software, or any portion thereof, without the written consent of Heaton Research, Inc. and the specific copyright owner(s) of any component software included on this media.

In the event that the Software or components include specific license requirements or end-user agreements, statements of condition, disclaimers, limitations or warranties ("End-User License"), those End-User Licenses supersede the terms and conditions herein as to that particular Software component. Your purchase, acceptance, or use of the Software will constitute your acceptance of such End-User Licenses.

By purchase, use or acceptance of the Software you further agree to comply with all export laws and regulations of the United States as such laws and regulations may exist from time to time.

SOFTWARE SUPPORT

Components of the supplemental Software and any offers associated with them may be supported by the specific Owner(s) of that material but they are not supported by Heaton Research, Inc.. Information regarding any available support may be obtained from the Owner(s) using the information provided in the appropriate README files or listed elsewhere on the media.

Should the manufacturer(s) or other Owner(s) cease to offer support or decline to honor any offer, Heaton Research, Inc. bears no responsibility. This notice concerning support for the Software is provided for your information only. Heaton Research, Inc. is not the agent or principal of the Owner(s), and Heaton Research, Inc. is in no way responsible for providing any support for the Software, nor is it liable or responsible for any support provided, or not provided, by the Owner(s).

WARRANTY

Heaton Research, Inc. warrants the enclosed media to be free of physical defects for a period of ninety (90) days after purchase. The Software is not available from Heaton Research, Inc. in any other form or media than that enclosed herein or posted to www.heatonresearch.com. If you discover a defect in the media during this warranty period, you may obtain a replacement of identical format at no charge by sending the defective media, postage prepaid, with proof of purchase to:

Heaton Research, Inc.
Customer Support Department
1734 Clarkson Rd #107
Chesterfield, MO 63017-4976
Web: www.heatonresearch.com
E-Mail: support@heatonresearch.com

DISCLAIMER

Heaton Research, Inc. makes no warranty or representation, either expressed or implied, with respect to the Software or its contents, quality, performance, merchantability, or fitness for a particular purpose. In no event will Heaton Research, Inc., its distributors, or dealers be liable to you or any other party for direct, indirect, special, incidental, consequential, or other damages arising out of the use of or inability to use the Software or its contents even if advised of the possibility of such damage. In the event that the Software includes an online update feature, Heaton Research, Inc. further disclaims any obligation to provide this feature for any specific duration other than the initial posting.

The exclusion of implied warranties is not permitted by some states. Therefore, the above exclusion may not apply to you. This warranty provides you with specific legal rights; there may be other rights that you may have that vary from state to state. The pricing of the book with the Software by Heaton Research, Inc. reflects the allocation of risk and limitations on liability contained in this agreement of Terms and Conditions.

SHAREWARE DISTRIBUTION

This Software may use various programs and libraries that are distributed as shareware. Copyright laws apply to both shareware and ordinary commercial software, and the copyright Owner(s) retains all rights. If you try a shareware program and continue using it, you are expected to register it. Individual programs differ on details of trial periods, registration, and payment. Please observe the requirements stated in appropriate files.

This book is dedicated to my wonderful wife, Tracy and our two cockatiels Cricket and Wynton.

Contents

Introduction

- Series Introduction

- Computer Languages

- Prerequisite Knowledge

- Fundamental Algorithms

- Other Resources

- Structure of this Book

This is the first in a series of books covering select topics in Artificial Intelligence (AI). Artificial Intelligence is a large field that encompasses many sub-disciplines. The following sections introduce both the series and the first volume.

0.1 Series Introduction

This series of books introduces the reader to a variety of popular topics in Artificial Intelligence. By no means is this meant to be an exhaustive AI resource–AI is a huge field, and a great deal of information is added on a daily basis. Each book focuses on a specific area of AI.

The series teaches Artificial Intelligence concepts in a mathematically gentle manner, which is why the series is named Artificial Intelligence for Humans. Still:

- I assume the reader is proficient in at least one programming language.

- I assume the reader has a basic understanding of college algebra.

- I use topics and formulas from calculus, linear algebra, differential equations, and statistics.

- However, when explaining topics in bullet point 3, I do not assume the reader is fluent in the topics described in the above bullet.

- I always follow concepts with real-world programming examples and pseudo code, rather than relying solely on mathematical formulas.

The target audience for this book comprises programmers who are proficient in at least one programming language. The book's examples have been ported to a number of programming languages.

0.1.1 Programming Languages

The actual book text stays at the pseudo code level. Example packs are provided for Java, C#, R, C/C++, and Python. There is also a community supplied port for the Scala programming language. Members of the community are working on porting the examples to additional languages, so your favorite language might have been ported since this printing. Check the book's GitHub repository for more information. The community is encouraged to help port to other languages! If you would like to get involved, your help would be greatly appreciated. Appendix A has more information to get you started.

0.1.2   Online Labs

Many of the examples from this series are available to run online, using HTML5. These examples use JavaScript and should run from mobile devices that are capable of HTML5.

All online lab materials can be found at the following web site:

http://www.aifh.org

These online labs allow you to try out examples even when reading an ebook from a mobile device.

0.1.3   Code Repositories

All of the code for this project is released under the Apache Open Source License v2. It can be found at the following GitHub repository:

https://github.com/jeffheaton/aifh

The online labs, with Javascript Lab Examples, can be found at the following GitHub repository:

https://github.com/jeffheaton/aifh-html

Have you found something broken, misspelled, or otherwise botched? You probably have. Fork the project and push a commit revision to GitHub. You will be credited among the growing number of contributors. Refer to Appendix A for more information on contributing code.

0.1.4   Books Planned for the Series

The following volumes are planned for this series:

- Volume 0: Introduction to the Math of AI

- Volume 1: Fundamental Algorithms

- Volume 2: Nature Inspired Algorithms

- Volume 3: Neural Networks

- Volume 4: Support Vector Machines

- Volume 5: Probabilistic Learning

Volumes one through five will be produced in order. Volume zero is a "planned prequel" that will be produced near the end of the series to focus on the mathematical concepts introduced in the other volumes. Volumes one through five will cover required mathematical concepts, while volume zero is planned to be a recap and expansion of the mathematical concepts from the other volumes.

Volume zero can be read at either the beginning or the end of the series. Volume one should generally be read before the other volumes. Volume two does contain some information useful for volume three. Figure 1 shows the suggested reading order.

Figure 1: Reading the Volumes

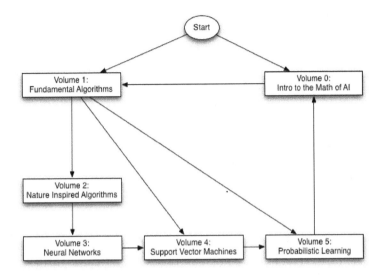

Each volume can be read separately or as part of the series. Volume one lays down foundational algorithms that are used in each of the subsequent volumes. The algorithms of volume one are both foundational and useful in their own right.

0.1.5   Other Resources

There are many other resources on the Internet that will be very useful to you as you read through this series of books.

The first is the Khan Academy, which is a collection of YouTube videos that demonstrate many areas of mathematics. If you need additional review on any mathematical concept in this book, there is most likely a video on the Khan Academy that covers it.

http://www.khanacademy.org/

Second is the Neural Network FAQ. This text-only resource has a great deal of information on neural networks and other AI topics.

http://www.faqs.org/faqs/ai-faq/neural-nets/

The Encog wiki has a fair amount of general information on machine learning, although the information found here is not necessarily tied to Encog.

http://www.heatonresearch.com/wiki/Main_Page

Finally, AI and neural networks can be discussed on the Encog forums. These forums are fairly active and you are very likely to receive an answer from myself or from one of the community members at the forum.

http://www.heatonresearch.com/forum

0.2 Fundamental Algorithms Introduction

To have a great building, you must have a great foundation. This book teaches Artificial Intelligence algorithms such as dimensionality, distance metrics, clustering, error calculation, hill climbing, linear regression and discrete learning. These algorithms allow for the processing and recognition of patterns in data. This is how sites such as Amazon and NetFlix suggest products to you.

These are not just foundational algorithms for the rest of the series, but are very useful algorithms in their own right. All algorithms are explained with numeric calculations that you can perform yourself.

0.3 Structure of this Book

Chapter one, "Introduction to AI," introduces some of the basic concepts of AI. These concepts are built upon both by this volume and the series. You will see that most AI algorithms accept an input array of numbers and produce an output array. Problems to be solved by AI are often modeled to this form. Internally, the algorithm keeps additional arrays that effectively represent long and short-term memory. These algorithms are trained by adjusting the long-term memory to produce a desirable output for a given input.

Chapter two, "Normalizing Data," shows how raw data is typically prepared for many AI algorithms. Data is presented to an algorithm in the form of an input array. Not all data is numeric and some is categorical. Examples of categorical data include color, shape, gender, species, and any other non-numeric descriptive quality. Numeric data must often be normalized to a specific range. Numeric qualities are often normalized to a range between -1 and 1.

Chapter three, "Distance Metrics," shows how data can be compared in much the same way as we plot a distance between two points on a map. AI often works with numeric arrays. These arrays hold input data, output data, long-term memory, short-term memory, and other information. These arrays are often called vectors. We can calculate the distances between these data points in much the same way as we calculate the distance between two points. Two-dimensional and three-dimensional points can be thought of as vectors of length two and three, respectively. In AI, we often deal with spaces of much higher dimensionality than three.

Chapter four, "Random Numbers," shows how random numbers are calculated and used by AI algorithms. This chapter begins by discussing the difference between uniform and normal random numbers. Sometimes AI algorithms call for each random number to have an equal probability. At other times, random numbers must follow a distribution. The chapter additionally discusses techniques for random number generation.

Chapter five, "K-Means Clustering," shows how data can be grouped into similar clusters. K-Means is an algorithm that can be used by itself to group data into groups by commonality. Additionally, K-Means is often used as a component to other more complex algorithms. Genetic algorithms often use K-Means to group populations into species with similar traits, while online retailers often use clustering algorithms to break customers into clusters. Sales suggestions can then be created based on the buying habits of members of the same cluster.

Chapter six, "Error Calculation," shows how the results of AI algorithms can be evaluated. Error calculation is how we determine the effectiveness of an algorithm, which can be done using a scoring function that evaluates the effectiveness of a trained algorithm. A very common type of scoring function simply contains input vectors and expected output vectors. This is called training data. The algorithm is rated based on the distance between the algorithm's actual output and the expected output.

Chapter seven, "Towards Machine Learning," introduces simple algorithms that can be trained to analyze data and produce better results. Most AI algorithms use a vector of weighted values to transform the input vector into a desired output vector. This vector of weighted values forms a sort of long-term memory for the algorithm. Training is the process of adjusting this memory to produce the desired output. This chapter shows how to construct several simple models that can be trained and introduces relatively simple, yet effective, training algorithms that can adjust this memory to provide better output values. Simple random walks and hill climbing are two such means for setting these weights.

Chapter eight, "Optimization Algorithms," expands the algorithms introduced in the previous chapter. These algorithms, which include Simulated Annealing and Nelder Mead, can be used to quickly optimize the weights of an AI model. This chapter shows how to adapt these optimization algorithms to some of the models introduced in the previous chapter.

Chapter nine, "Discrete Optimization," shows how to optimize data that is categorical rather than numeric. Not every optimization problem is numeric, as we see in the cases of discrete, or categorical, problems such as the Knapsack Problem and the Traveling Salesman Problem. This chapter shows that Simulated Annealing can be adapted to either of these two problems. Simulated annealing can be used for continuous numeric problems and discrete categorical problems.

Chapter ten, "Linear Regression," shows how linear and non-linear equations can be used to learn trends and make predictions. The chapter introduces simple linear regression and shows how to use it to fit data to a linear model. This chapter will also introduce the General Linear Model (GLM), which can be used to fit non-linear data.

0.4   The Kickstarter Campaign

This series of books was launched in 2013 as the result of a successful Kickstarter campaign. The home page for the Kickstarter project is shown in Figure 2.

Figure 2: The Kickstarter Campaign

You can visit the original Kickstarter at the following link:

http://goo.gl/dGorA

I would like to thank all of the Kickstarter backers of the project! Without your support, this series might not exist. I would also like to extend a special thanks to those backers who supported at the $100 and higher levels. They are listed here, in order that they pledged.

Figure 3: Kickstarter 100 Dollar Level Supporters

Dr. Warren D. Lerner
Dave Snell
Oyvind R Lorentzen
Jeffrey Elrod
Anders Steffen Öding Andersen
Rick Cardarelle
Andy Eunson
Tracy Turnage Heaton
Davíð Helgason
Patrick Saint - laurent
Bradford Nazario Barr
Chris Duesing
Arsham Hatambeiki
Alex Brem
Randy J. Ray
Matthew Schissler
Matthew March
Yvonne Norton Leung
Travis Thaxton

Also a big thanks to Rick Cardarelle! His pledge of $358 pushed the project to the $2,500 minimum requested amount. A very big thank you to Rory Graves and Matic Potocnik porting the examples to Scala.

Thank you everyone–you are the best!

Chapter 1

Introduction to AI

- Relationship to Human Brains

- Modeling Input and Output

- Classification and Regression

- Time Series

- Training

Most laypeople think of Artificial Intelligence (AI) as a sort of artificial brain and recall images from science fiction movies about robots. Such images have very little to do with how AI is actually used in today's world. It is true that AI has many similarities to human brain function, but the significant distinction is that Artificial Intelligence is artificial. AI does not need to pretend to be biological.

Before we get too deep, I would like to introduce some very general concepts about how you interact with an AI algorithm. The AI algorithm is the technique that you are using to solve a problem. An AI algorithm is sometimes called a model. There are many different AI algorithms, or models. Some of the most common are Neural Networks, Support Vector Machines, Bayesian networks, and Hidden Markov Models. This series of books covers many of these models.

It is important for the AI practitioner understand how to represent a problem to an AI program, as this is the primary mode of interaction with an AI algorithm. We will begin our foundation of knowledge in this topic by exploring how the human brain interacts with its world.

1.1   Relationship to Human Brains

The purpose of AI is to allow a computer to function somewhat like a human brain. However, this does not mean that AI seeks to emulate every aspect of the human brain. The degree to which an AI algorithm matches the actual functioning of the human brain is called biological plausibility.

Christof Koch, chief scientific officer of the Allen Institute for Brain Science, calls the brain "the most complex object in the known universe." (Koch, 2013) In the context of AI, the brain is essentially an advanced piece of technology that we must study, reverse engineer, and learn to emulate.

The brain is not the only piece of "advanced technology" that nature has shared with us. Flight is another. Early airplanes attempted to emulate the flapping wings of birds. Such airships are called ornithopters. These flapping airships did not work very well, however. Figure 1.1 shows a patent diagram for the Gray Goose Ornithopter.

Figure 1.1: Gray Goose Ornithopter (US patent 1,730,758)

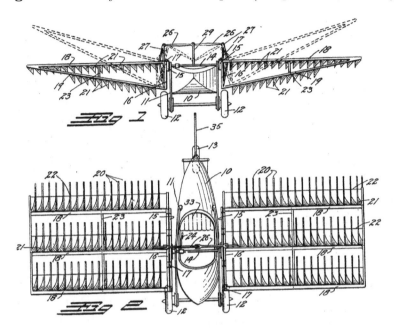

Biological birds were the only models for flying machines in existence through the early 1900s. It seemed logical to emulate birds, as they were excellent flyers. However, from experimenting with flying machines, humans have learned not to follow the path of nature too closely. While we wanted to emulate the end goal of flying, emulating exactly how natural bird flight occurs did not result in an effective flying machine.

The abstraction of emulation occurs in many other contexts. My MacBook Pro can emulate a Windows PC, and can also emulate a Commodore 64 (C64). A C64 is somewhat different from my more modern laptop, in more than just looks. The instruction set that drives a C64 is quite different from the Intel x86 instruction set common on many modern computers. When my Mac emulates a C64, it does not emulate the actual transistors that make up a C64's 6510 microprocessor. The emulation occurs at a higher level. This is the same in AI. Some algorithms emulate neurons, while some, like my C64 emulator, operate at a higher level. We focus on the end goal of providing functionality in a PC context, rather than directly emulating all the processes that lead to functionality in a brain.

What you want to do is more important than how. At the highest level, there are similarities between a human brain and most AI algorithms. The next section will examine these.

1.1.1   The Brain and Its World

Before we begin, let's look at how the human brain works on an external level. While we know relatively little about the internal operation of the brain, we do know a fair amount about the external operation of the brain.

The brain is essentially a black box connected by nerves. These nerves carry signals between the brain and the body. A certain set of inputs causes a certain output. For example, feeling your finger about to touch a hot stove will result in other nerves sending commands to your muscles to pull your finger back.

It is also very important to note that the brain has an internal state. Consider if you suddenly heard a horn. How you react is determined not just by the stimuli of the horn, but where you are when you hear the horn. Hearing a horn in the middle of a movie evokes a very different response than hearing a horn when you are crossing a busy street. The knowledge of where you are creates a certain internal state that causes your brain to react differently to different contexts.

The order in which stimuli are received is also important. A common game is to close your eyes and attempt to use only touch to determine what an object is. When you grab the object, you do not instantly receive enough information to determine what it is. Rather, you must grab the object and run your fingers over it. As your fingers run over the object, you receive information that forms an image of what the object is.

You can essentially think of the human brain as a black box with a series of inputs and outputs. Our nerves provide our entire perception of the world. The nerves are the inputs to the brain. There is actually a finite number of inputs to a typical human brain.

Likewise, our only means to interact with the world are the outputs from our nerves to our muscles. The output from the human brain is a function of the inputs and internal state of the brain. In response to any input, the human brain will alter its internal state and produce output. The significance of the order of the inputs is handled by the internal state of the brain.

1.1.2 Brain in a Vat

If our only interaction with reality is the inputs we receive from sensory inputs and out actions through motor nerves, what actually is "reality"? Your brain is hooked up to your body, but it could also be hooked up to a simulation, as in the movie, The Matrix. So long as the output from your brain is producing the expected inputs, would you know what was real and what was simulated?

This is a common philosophical thought experiment called "brain in a vat." Figure 1.2 illustrates the brain in a vat thought experiment. In the figure, the brain believes that its body is walking a dog. But does the brain have a body? Does the dog even exist? What does "exist" even mean? All we really know is what our nerves tell us. (Sigiel, 1999)

Figure 1.2: Brain in a Vat

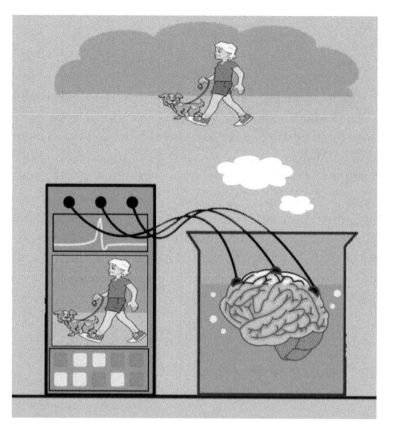

This experiment assumes that a person's brain could be removed from the body and provided life-support. Nerves would be connected to a super-computer that would provide electrical impulses identical to those the brain normally receives. The computer would then be simulating reality by including appropriate responses to the brain's output. The disembodied brain would continue to have perfectly normal conscious experiences outside of the "real world." There are even philosophical theories that suggest we are living in a simulation. (Bostrom, 2003)

One attempt to model an algorithm directly from the human brain is the neural network. Neural networks are one small part of AI research, and the neural network model aligns very closely with many of the AI algorithms that you will learn in this series of books.

Computer based neural networks are not like the human brain in that they are not general-purpose computation devices. Neural networks, as they currently exist, carry out very small, specific tasks. An AI algorithm experiences its reality by providing output based on the algorithm's internal state and the input it is currently receiving. The "reality" that the algorithm is attached to may change as the researcher experiments with the algorithm.

This model of inputs, outputs, and internal state holds true for most AI algorithms, regardless of whether you are creating AI for a robot or a stock picker. Of course, some algorithms are more complex than others.

1.2   Modeling Problems

Knowing how to model a real-world problem to a machine-learning algorithm is critical. Different problems will lend themselves to different algorithms. At the highest level, you will model your problem in one of four different ways:

- Data classification

- Regression analysis

- Clustering

- Time Series

Sometimes you will model one problem using several of these approaches. We will examine each of these, beginning with data classification.

1.2.1   Data Classification

Classification attempts to determine the class in which the input data falls into. Classification is usually a supervised training operation, which occurs when the user provides data and expected results to the machine-learning algorithm. In data classification, the expected result is identification of the data class.

Supervised training always deals with known data. During training, machine-learning algorithms are evaluated according to how well they classify known data. The hope is that the algorithm, once trained, will be able to classify unknown data as well.

Fisher's Iris Dataset is an example of classification. (Fisher, 1936) This dataset contains measurements of iris flowers. This is one of the most famous datasets and is often used to evaluate machine-learning algorithms. The full dataset is available at the following URL:

http://www.heatonresearch.com/wiki/Iris_Data_Set

Below is a small sampling from the iris dataset.

```
"Sepal Length","Sepal Width","Petal Length","Petal Width","Species
    "
5.1,3.5,1.4,0.2,"setosa"
4.9,3.0,1.4,0.2,"setosa"
4.7,3.2,1.3,0.2,"setosa"
...
7.0,3.2,4.7,1.4,"versicolor"
6.4,3.2,4.5,1.5,"versicolor"
6.9,3.1,4.9,1.5,"versicolor"
...
6.3,3.3,6.0,2.5,"virginica"
5.8,2.7,5.1,1.9,"virginica"
7.1,3.0,5.9,2.1,"virginica"
```

The above data are shown as a Comma Separated Value (CSV) file. CSV is a very common input format for machine learning. The first row is typically a definition for each of the columns in the file. As you can see, for each of the flowers there are five pieces of information provided:

- Sepal length

- Sepal width

- Petal length

- Petal width

- Species

For classification, the algorithm is instructed to determine the species of the flower given the sepal length/width and the petal length/width. The species is the class.

A class is usually a non-numeric data attribute and, as such, membership in the class must be well defined. For the Iris dataset, there are three different types of iris. If a machine-learning algorithm is trained on three types of iris, it cannot be expected to identify a rose. All members of the class must be known at the time of training.

1.2.2   Regression Analysis

In the last section, we learned how to use data to classify data. But often the desired output is not simply a class, but a number. Consider the calculation of an automobile's fuel efficiency in miles per gallon (MPG). Provided data such as the engine size and car weight, the MPG for the specified car may be calculated.

The following sample provides MPG data for five cars:

```
"mpg","cylinders","displacement","horsepower","weight","
    acceleration","model year","origin","car name"
18.0,8,307.0,130.0,3504.,12.0,70,1,"chevrolet chevelle malibu"
15.0,8,350.0,165.0,3693.,11.5,70,1,"buick skylark 320"
18.0,8,318.0,150.0,3436.,11.0,70,1,"plymouth satellite"
16.0,8,304.0,150.0,3433.,12.0,70,1,"amc rebel sst"
17.0,8,302.0,140.0,3449.,10.5,70,1,"ford torino"
...
```

The entirety of this dataset may be found at the link below: (Quinlan, 1993)

http://www.heatonresearch.com/wiki/MPG_Data_Set

A regression analysis aims to train the algorithm with input data about the car to provide an answer calculated from input. In this case, the algorithm would be asked to determine the miles per gallon that the specified car would likely get.

It is also important to note that not every piece of data in the above file will be used. The columns "car name" and "origin" are not used. The name of a car has nothing to do with its fuel efficiency and is therefore excluded from the calculation. Likewise, the origin of the car does not contribute to this equation. Although the origin is given a numeric value that specifies what geographic region the car was produced in and some regions do focus more on fuel efficiency than others, this piece of data is far too broad to be useful.

1.2.3   Clustering

Clustering is very similar to classification in that the computer is required to group data. Clustering algorithms take input data and place it into clusters. The programmer usually specifies the number of clusters to be created before training the algorithm. The computer places similar items together using the input data. Because you do not specify what cluster you expect a given item to fall into, clustering is useful when you have no expected output. Because there is no expected output, clustering is considered unsupervised training.

Consider the car data from the previous section. You might run a clustering algorithm to break the cars into four groups. This would tell you what cars are similar to each other.

The difference between clustering and classification is that clustering gives the algorithm the freedom to find order in the data. Classification teaches the algorithm what class known data should fit into, with the goal of allowing the trained algorithm to eventually classify new data that the algorithm was not trained with.

Clustering and classification algorithms handle new data differently. The entire purpose of classification is to be able to classify new data based on previous data with which the algorithm was trained, while clustering makes no provision for new data. If you want to add new data to the existing groups, you must recluster the entire data set.

1.2.4 Time Series

Machine learning algorithms work somewhat like mathematical functions. They map the input values to output values. If there is no internal state to the machine-learning algorithm, a given set of inputs will always produce the same outputs. Many machine-learning methods do not have an internal state that changes and affects the output. For example, in the context of the car data, you would want the classification algorithm's decision to be supported by all the data, rather than just by the last few cars that it has seen.

Time series is often very important. Some machine-learning algorithms support it and others do not. If you are classifying cars or irises you most likely do not care about time series. However, if your only input is the current price of a stock, time series becomes very important. A single price point for a stock on a given day does not help much for prediction. However, a trend considering several days of stock prices may be of use.

There are also methods to encode time series into algorithms that do not directly support time series. In these cases you make the previous days part of the input. For example, you may have five inputs that represent the previous five days of trading from the day you wish to predict.

1.3   Modeling Input and Output

Earlier in this chapter I mentioned that a machine-learning algorithm is provided with input and produces output. This output is affected by the algorithm's long- and short-term memory. Figure 1.3 shows how long- and short-term memory are involved in the output process.

Figure 1.3: Abstract Machine Learning Algorithm

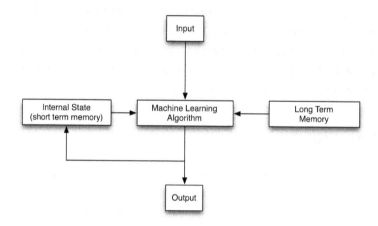

As you can see, the algorithm above accepts input and produces output. Most machine learning algorithms operate completely synchronously. The algorithm will only output when presented with input. It is not like a human brain, which always responds to input but occasionally produces output without input!

So far we have only referred to the input and output patterns abstractly. You may be wondering exactly what they are. The input and output patterns are both vectors. A vector is essentially an array of floating point numbers, as shown below:

```
Input:  [ -0.245, .283, 0.0 ]
Output: [ 0.782, 0.543 ]
```

Nearly all machine learning algorithms have a fixed number of inputs and outputs. They work like functions in computer programs. The input can be thought of as the parameters to a function. The output is the return value. For the above data an algorithm would accept three input values and return two output values. These counts do not typically change. As a result, the number of elements in the input and output patterns for a particular algorithm can never change.

To make use of the algorithm, you must express your problem in such a way as to have the input to the problem be an array of floating point numbers. Likewise, the solution to the problem must be an array of floating point numbers. This is really all that most algorithms can do for you. Machine learning algorithms take one array and transform it into a second.

Many pattern recognition algorithms are something like a hash table in traditional programming. In traditional programming, a hash table is used to map keys to values. In many ways, a hash table is somewhat like a dictionary, in that it includes a term and its meaning. A hash table could look like the following:

- "hear" -> "to perceive or apprehend by the ear"

- "run" -> "to go faster than a walk"

- "write" -> "to form (as characters or symbols) on a surface with an instrument (as a pen)"

The above example is a mapping between words and their definitions. This hash table uses a key of the data type string and applies it to another value of a string. If you provide the dictionary with a key (the word), it returns a value (the definition). This is how most machine learning algorithms function.

All program hash tables use keys and values. Think of the pattern sent to the input layer of the algorithm as the key to the hash table. Likewise, think of the value returned from the hash table as the pattern that is returned from the output layer of the algorithm. Of course, an algorithm is much more than a simple hash table.

With the above hash table, what would happen if you were to pass in a word that is not a key in the map? For example, the key "wrote." A hash table would return null or in some way indicate that it could not find the specified key. Machine learning algorithms, on the other hand, do not return null. They find the closest match, or a probability of a match. If you passed "wrote" to the algorithm above, you would likely get back what you would have expected for "write."

Not only does the algorithm find the closest match, it will modify the output to guess the missing value. Of course, there is not enough data for the algorithm to have modified the response in the example above, as there are only three samples. When the data is limited the closest match may not be very meaningful.

The above mapping brings up one very important point about these algorithms. Given that algorithms accept an array of floating point numbers and return another array, how would you put strings into the algorithm? There is a way to do this, although it is much easier to deal with numeric data than strings.

The Bag of Words algorithm is a common means of encoding strings. (Harris, 1954) Each input represents the count of one particular word. The entire input vector would contain one value for each unique word. Consider the following strings.

```
Of Mice and Men
Three Blind Mice
Blind Man's Bluff
Mice and More Mice
```

We have the following unique words. This is our "dictionary."

```
Input 0: and
Input 1: blind
Input 2: bluff
Input 3: man's
Input 4: men
Input 5: mice
Input 6: more
Input 7: of
Input 8: three
```

The four lines above would be encoded as follows.

```
Of Mice and Men [0 4 5 7]
Three Blind Mice [1 5 8]
Blind Man's Bluff [1 2 3]
Mice and More Mice [0 5 6]
```

Of course we have to fill in the missing words with zero, so we end up with the following.

```
Of Mice and Men [1, 0, 0, 0, 1, 1, 0, 1, 0]
Three Blind Mice [0, 1, 0, 0, 0, 1, 0, 0, 1]
Blind Man's Bluff [0, 1, 1, 1, 0, 0, 0, 0, 0]
Mice and More Mice [1, 0, 0, 0, 0, 2, 1, 0, 0]
```

Notice that we now have a consistent vector length of nine. Nine is the total number of words in our "dictionary". Each component number in the vector is an index into our dictionary of available words. At each vector component is stored a count of the number of words for that dictionary entry. Each string will usually contain only a small subset of the dictionary. As a result, most of the vector values will be zero.

As you can see, one of the most difficult aspects of machine learning programming is translating your problem into a fixed-length array of floating point numbers. The following section shows how to translate several examples.

1.3.1   A Simple Example

If you have read anything about machine learning, you have no doubt seen examples with the Exclusive Or (XOR) operator. A program learning the **XOR** operator is essentially the "Hello World" of AI. This book will describe scenarios much more complex than **XOR**, but the **XOR** operator is a great introduction. We shall begin by looking at the **XOR** operator as though it were a hash table. If you are not familiar with the **XOR** operator, it works similarly to the **AND** and **OR** operators in that it considers two sides and generates a **true** or **false** answer. An **AND** operator is **true** when both sides are **true**. Likewise an **OR** is **true** when either side is **true**.

For an **XOR** to be **true**, both of the sides must be different from each other. The truth table for an **XOR** is as follows.

```
False XOR False = False
True XOR False = True
False XOR True = True
True XOR True = False
```

The above truth table would be represented in hash table form as follows:

```
[ 0.0 , 0.0 ] -> [ 0.0 ]
[ 1.0 , 0.0 ] -> [ 1.0 ]
[ 0.0 , 1.0 ] -> [ 1.0 ]
[ 1.0 , 1.0 ] -> [ 0.0 ]
```

These mappings show the input and the ideal expected output for the algorithm.

1.3.2 Miles per Gallon

Machine learning problems usually involve dealing with a set of data and using a calculation to predict the output data or to determine a course of action. Consider a car database that contains the following fields:

- Car weight

- Engine displacement

- Cylinder count

- Horse power

- Hybrid or gasoline

- Miles per gallon

Assuming you have collected some data for these fields, you should be able to construct a model that can predict one field value based on the other field values. For this example, we will try to predict miles per gallon.

We will need to define this problem in terms of an input array of floating point values mapped to an output array of floating point values. Furthermore, the numeric range on each of these array elements should be between 0 and 1 or -1 and 1. This is called normalization. Normalization will be covered in much greater detail in the next chapter.

First, we see how we would normalize data from above. Consider the input and output data formats. We have six total fields. We want to use five of these to predict the sixth. The algorithm would have five inputs and one output.

Your algorithm's input and output would look something like the following.

- Input 1: Car weight

- Input 2: Engine displacement

- Input 3: Cylinder count

- Input 4: Horse power

- Input 5: Hybrid or gasoline

- Output 1: Miles per gallon

We also need to normalize the data. To do this we must think of reasonable ranges for each of these values. We will then transform input data into a number between 0 and 1 that represents an actual value's position within that range. The following example establishes reasonable ranges for these values:

- Car weight: 100-5000 lbs

- Engine displacement: 0.1-10 liters

- Cylinder count: 2-12

- Horse power: 1-1000

- Hybrid or gasoline: true or false

- Miles per gallon: 1-500

These ranges may be a little large for modern cars. However, this will allow minimal restructuring to the algorithm in the future. It is also best to use ranges that will not invite too much data at their extreme ends, so a large range is best.

We will now look at an example. How would we normalize a weight of 2,000 pounds? This weight is 1,900 into the range and the size of the range is 4,900 pounds. The percent of the range size is 0.38 (1,900 / 4,900). Therefore, we would feed the value of 0.38 to the algorithm input to represent this value. This satisfies the typical range requirement of 0 to 1 for an input.

The hybrid or regular value is a true/false. To represent this value we will use 1 for hybrid and 0 for regular. We simply normalize a true/false into two values.

1.3.3   Presenting Images to Algorithms

Images are a popular source of input for algorithms. In this section, we will see how to normalize an image. There are more advanced methods than this, but this method is often effective.

Consider a full-color image of 300x300 pixels. 90,000 pixels times the three RGB colors gives 270,000 total pixels. If we had an input for each pixel, that would be 270,000 inputs. This is just too large for many algorithms.

Thus, we need to downsample. Consider the following image, which is at full resolution (Figure 1.4).

Figure 1.4: An Image at Full Resolution

We will now downsample it to 32x32, as shown below (Figure 1.5).

Figure 1.5: An Image Downsampled

The grid-like pattern of the image after it has been reduced to 32x32 pixels allows us to use the pixels to form the input to an algorithm. This algorithm would require 1,024 inputs, if the algorithm were to only look at the intensity of each square. Looking at the intensity causes the algorithm to "see" in black and white.

If you would like the algorithm to see in color, then it is necessary to provide the intensity of red, green, and blue (RGB) values for each of these pixels. This would mean three inputs for each pixel, which would push our input count to 3,072.

The normal intensity range for RGB values is between 0 and 255. To create input for the algorithm, simply divide the intensity by 255 to create an intensity percentage. For example, intensity number 10 becomes 10/255, or 0.039.

You may be wondering how the outputs will be handled. In a case such as this, the outputs should communicate what image the algorithm believes it is looking at. The usual solution is to create one output for each type of image the algorithm should recognize. The algorithm will be trained to return a value of 1.0 for the output that corresponds to what the image is believed to be.

We will continue showing you how to format algorithms for real-world problems in the next section, which will take a look at financial algorithms.

1.3.4   Financial Algorithms

Financial forecasting is a very popular form of temporal algorithm. A temporal algorithm is one that accepts input for values that range over time. If the algorithm supports short term memory (internal state) then ranges over time are supported automatically. If your algorithm does not have an internal state then you should use an input window and a prediction window. Most algorithms do not have an internal state. To see how to use these windows, consider if you would like the algorithm to predict the stock market. You begin with the closing price for a stock over several days.

```
Day 1:  $45
Day 2:  $47
Day 3:  $48
Day 4:  $40
Day 5:  $41
Day 6:  $43
Day 7:  $45
Day 8:  $57
Day 9:  $50
Day 10: $41
```

The first step is to normalize the data. This is necessary whether your algo-rithm has internal state or not. To normalize, we want to change each number into the percent movement from the previous day. For example, day 2 would become 0.04, because there is a 4% difference between $45 and $47. Once you perform this calculation for every day, the data set will look like the following:

```
Day 2:  0.04
Day 3:  0.02
Day 4: −0.16
Day 5:  0.02
Day 6:  0.04
Day 7:  0.04
Day 8:  0.04
Day 9: −0.12
Day 10: −0.18
```

In order to create an algorithm that will predict the next day's values, we need to think about how to encode this data to be presented to the algorithm. The encoding depends on whether the algorithm has an internal state. The internal state allows the algorithm to use the last few values inputted to help establish trends.

Many machine learning algorithms have no internal state. If this is the case, then you will typically use a sliding window algorithm to encode the data. To do this, we use the last three prices to predict the next one. The inputs would be the last three-day prices, and the output would be the fourth day. The above data could be organized in the following way to provide training data. These cases specified the ideal output for the given inputs.

```
[0.04 ,0.02 ,−0.16]  −>  0.02
[0.02 ,−0.16 ,0.02]  −>  0.04
[−0.16 ,0.02 ,0.04]  −>  0.04
[0.02 ,0.04 ,0.04]   −>  0.04
[0.04 ,0.04 ,0.04]   −>  −0.12
[0.04 ,0.04 ,−0.12]  −>  −0.18
```

The above encoding would require that the algorithm have three inputs and one output.

1.4   Understanding Training

What exactly is training? Training is the process whereby an algorithm is adapted for the training data. This can be different from the "internal state" that I have mentioned. You can think of training as affecting the long-term memory of an algorithm. For a neural network, training is the weight matrix.

When training occurs depends on the algorithm. Usually, training and actual usage of the algorithm are divided into two distinct phases. Sometimes, training and usage can occur simultaneously.

1.4.1   Evaluating Success

In school, students are graded as they learn their subjects. There are many purposes for these grades. The most basic purpose is to provide the student with feedback on their path of learning. You must also evaluate your algorithms as they train. This evaluation will both guide the training and provide you feedback as to the success of the training.

One method of evaluation is to provide a scoring function. This scoring function takes a trained algorithm and evaluates it. The scoring function simply returns a score. The goal will be to either minimize or maximize this score. Whether any given problem is a minimization or maximization problem is purely arbitrary and is the preference of the scoring programming.

1.4.2 Batch and Online Training

Batch and online training usually come into play when you are dealing with a training set, as they refer to types of learning processes. For online training, learning occurs after each training set element. Batch training accumulates learning from a certain number of elements and then the algorithm is updated accordingly. The designated number of elements is called the batch size. Often, the batch size is equal to the total training size.

Online training can be useful when an algorithm must learn and train at the same time. The human brain always works in this mode. However, online training is less common in AI, and not all algorithms support online training. Online training support is very common for neural networks, however.

1.4.3 Supervised and Unsupervised Training

This chapter outlines two different training methods: supervised and unsupervised. Supervised training occurs when you know the output that you desire from the algorithm. Unsupervised training occurs when you do not provide the expected outputs to the algorithm.

There are also hybrid-training methods. In a hybrid training method, you provide only some expected outputs. This training method is used with deep belief neural networks.

1.4.4 Stochastic and Deterministic Training

A deterministic training algorithm always performs exactly the same way, given the same initial state. There are typically no random numbers used in a deterministic training algorithm.

Stochastic training makes use of random numbers. Because of this, an algorithm will always train differently, even with the same starting state. This can make it difficult to evaluate the effectiveness of a stochastic algorithm. However, stochastic algorithms are very common and very effective.

1.5   Chapter Summary

This chapter provided a basic introduction to AI, particularly machine learning. You saw how problems are modeled to a machine-learning algorithm. Machine learning algorithms share some similarities to biological processes, but the goal of AI is not to exactly emulate the workings of a human brain. The goal of machine learning is to produce machines capable of some degree of intelligence beyond simple procedural programming.

Machine learning is similar to the human brain in that there is input, output, and potentially an internal state. The input and internal state determine what the output will be. This internal state can be thought of as a short-term memory that influences the output. There is also a long term memory that dictates exactly what the machine learning algorithm will output given the input and internal state. Training is the process of adjusting this long-term memory so that the machine learning algorithm produces the desired output.

Machine learning algorithms are typically broken into several groups: regression and classification algorithms. Regression algorithms will output a number given one or more inputs. Regression algorithms are essentially multivariate functions. These algorithms accept several inputs and produce an output of one or more values.

Classification algorithms accept one or more variable to return a single class instance. They are allowed to make decisions based on the input. For example, a classification algorithm might be used to sort job applicants into preferred, average, and denied groups.

This chapter showed that the input to a machine learning algorithm is a vector of numbers. It is important to understand how to represent problems as a vector of numbers in order to pose your question to the algorithm.

The next chapter will introduce normalization. Normalization broadly refers to the means by which data are prepared to become input for a machine learning algorithm. Additionally, normalization is used to interpret the output from the machine learning algorithm.

Chapter 2

Normalization

- What is Normalization?

- Reciprocal Normalization and Denormalization

- Range Normalization and Denormalization

In the last chapter, we saw that a machine-learning algorithm is given a vector of floating point numbers. This is the input vector. We also saw that the machine-learning algorithm would return a vector in response to the input. This is the output vector.

This chapter looks at how to present data as an input vector, as well as how to interpret the results from the output vector. In order to do so, we must learn about the several different types of data, which are all normalized in different ways.

2.1 Levels of Measurement

In statistics, data is typically broken down into two major categories: qualitative and quantitative. In general, quantitative data deals with quantities, or numbers. Qualitative data deals with qualities, or descriptions.

For example, consider a cup of coffee. You could describe the coffee both qualitatively and quantitatively. If you were to describe the cup of coffee qualitatively, you might list the following attributes:

- Brown

- Strong aroma

- White cup

- Hot to the touch

These are all non-numerical qualities, and thus are qualitative. You can also describe the cup of coffee quantitatively.

- 12 fluid ounces

- 106 calories

- 65 degrees Celsius

- $4.99 cost

These are all numeric quantities that describe the cup of coffee.

We can describe the types of data in even greater detail by categorizing them into one of four subcategories. These data types were defined by psychologist Stanley Smith Stevens in the article "On the Theory of Scales of Measurement." (Stevens, 1946) These four data types are as follows:

- Nominal data

- Ordinal data

- Interval data

- Ratio data

Nominal and ordinal observations are both qualitative, while interval and ratio observations are both quantitative. The differences between each of the four can be somewhat confusing. I prefer to think of them in terms of what basic mathematical operations can be used with each. This is summarized in Figure 2.1.

Figure 2.1: Levels of Measurement

	Nominal	Ordinal	Interval	Ratio
* or /	No	No	No	Yes
+ or -	No	No	Yes	Yes
< or >	No	Yes	Yes	Yes
= or ! =	Yes	Yes	Yes	Yes
Example	Gender	Hot/warm/cold	Year	Age

You can usually determine the type of observation by considering what operators are valid on it. For example, if you have two colors, you can determine whether the two colors are equal (that is, whether both are the same color). One color is not greater than another color, however. You can't add two colors, nor can you multiply two colors. Given these properties, colors are nominal.

Now let's consider ordinals. The observation that something is hot or warm indicates an implied ordering; the "hotness" of a cup of coffee is ordinal. Given two cups of coffee, one can determine whether they are the same degree of hotness and whether one is hotter than the other. Ordinals are not only ordered, but the levels of order are clearly defined. In the case of the levels of "hotness," levels include scalding, hot, warm, room temperature, and cold.

For a slightly more complex example of nominal and ordinal observations, consider a zip code such as those used in the United States to allow for the quick sorting of letters and packages. They are made up of six digits, and each specifies a particular region. For example, the 90210 zip code specifies an address in Beverly Hills, California.

Although zip codes are always made up of digits and look like numbers, they are not numbers. You could compare two zip codes to see if they are equal, but to add to or subtract from a zip code would give a meaningless answer. So a zip code is clearly qualitative, rather than quantitative. But is it nominal or ordinal? Although one could compare the numerical value of zip codes to say that one zip code is greater than another, the higher value of a zip code gives it no special meaning. Certainly, higher zip codes are often in the west of the USA and lower zip codes often specify a location in the east, but this tendency does not hold true in all cases. Zip codes, therefore, are nominal.

2.1.1 Quantitative Observations

Now we will look at quantitative observations. The relationship between interval and ratio can be a little more complex than between ordinal and nominal. In addition to the operators above, I will give you one additional rule to define the difference. Interval observations have an arbitrary zero, whereas ratio observations have an actual non-arbitrary zero that defines their beginning.

For example, age is a ratio. It has a clearly defined origin at zero, for there are no ages before age 0. The current year, on the other hand, is an interval. It does not have a clearly defined origin at 0.

Let's apply the operator test to these two examples. You can say that someone is twice the age of someone else, so the multiplier rule is a yes, which defines age as a ratio. You could treat the current year as a number and multiply it by 2, but that would not mean that one date was twice the other, because dates do not have an origin at 0. However, you may add and subtract quantities from dates to get meaning, so the current date does count as an interval.

Temperature can be either a ratio or an interval, depending on the scale used. If you measure the temperature in Kelvin, then zero is absolute zero; thus, temperature measured in Kelvin is a ratio. Temperature measured in Fahrenheit or Celsius is an interval, on the other hand, because zero is not the origin for either Fahrenheit or Celsius.

Test this definition using the phrase "twice as hot." Ten degrees Celsius cannot be twice as hot as five degrees Celsius. Thus, because the term "twice" has no meaning with Celsius or Fahrenheit, they are intervals rather than ratios.

With Kelvin, zero is absolute zero–there is no molecular movement at all, and it cannot possibly be colder than 0. In the case of Kelvin, 0 is the true origin point. Twice as hot as 5 is in fact 10 degrees, in Kelvin.

Similarly, speeds are ratios: twice as fast as five kilometers per hour is ten kilometers per hour. There is no going slower than zero kilometers per hour, and so zero is the true origin point.

Most scientific measurements are ratio observations. These include length, width, electrical charge, volume, mass, and Kelvin temperature. The value of interval measurements are still helpful trackers, but typically their meaning is more arbitrary.

2.2   Normalizing Observations

In the previous chapter we saw that all input and output from machine learning algorithms are typically vectors of floating point numbers. The real world observations that we provide to a machine learning algorithm must be nominal, ordinal, interval, or ratio. Nominal and ordinal observations are not inherently numeric, so we need to convert these into a number that is meaningful to the machine learning algorithm.

Some machine learning algorithms require that all observations be in a specific range, usually -1 to +1 or 0 to +1. Even if you are not required to be in a specific range, it is often a good idea to ensure that your values fall into a range. This will normalize the values so they can be compared.

Why is normalization necessary? Consider if you made two observations, one of which was the daily volume of the NYSE and the other of which was the point movement of an individual stock. The NYSE daily volume is usually in the billions, while the number of points moved by many individual stocks is typically less than 10. The volume number could easily overwhelm the point movement, making the point movement seem meaningless, or zero.

Normalization is something we see every day. One of its most common forms is that of percentages. If something is 5% off, you can easily tell the relative size of the discount. It might be a few dollars for a new cell phone or it might be several hundred dollars for a car, yet the size of the percentage figure stays the same. We could normalize the values in the NYSE example by considering them as percentages. Now we might say that the volume increased by 10%, while the stock fell by 5%. The volume number is now comparable to the point number.

In the next sections we will see how to normalize nominal, ordinal, interval, and ratio observations.

2.2.1   Normalizing Nominal Observations

There are two commonly used methods for normalizing ordinal values. In this section, we will look at one-of-n encoding. This the most simple means of normalizing nominal values. Later in this chapter, we will discuss equilateral encoding. Equilateral encoding is more complex, but is often more efficient than one-of-n encoding.

One-of-n is a very simple form of normalization. For an example, consider the iris dataset that we saw in the last chapter. A single line from the iris data set is shown here. The species is non-numeric. We will have to use one-of-n normalization for it.

```
5.1 ,3.5 ,1.4 ,0.2 ,Iris −setosa
```

The first four values are all ratio observations, as they are lengths and the origin is at zero. However, the fifth value is nominal, which is sometimes called categorical. It describes a category. The nominal value is defined by the species of the iris; in the iris dataset described above, there were three iris species:

- Setosa

- Versicolor

- Virginica

With the one-of-n normalization, the machine learning algorithm would have three outputs–one for each iris species. The machine learning algorithm would most likely be trained to accept the four length measurements as inputs and then output three values to predict what species of iris the input data corresponds to.

Normalization is used to create training data. A machine learning algorithm is trained with training data. The actual process of training will be covered later in this book. For now, you simply need to be aware that a training set is a collection of input vectors that includes the ideal output for each vector. We can use the iris data set to generate a training set. First, to generate the inputs, we will normalize each of the four ratio observations. Later in the chapter we will see how to normalize ratio observations. For now, we will focus on the species.

Generating the ideal output for each of these input vectors is relatively easy. Simply assign a +1 to the neuron that corresponds to the chosen iris and a -1 to the remaining neurons. For example, using a normalization range of -1 to 1, the Setosa iris species would be encoded as follows:

```
1,−1,−1
```

Likewise, the Versicolor would be encoded as follows:

```
−1,1,−1
```

Finally, Virginica would be encoded as follows.

```
−1,−1,1
```

If you are using 0 to 1, then substitute 0 for the -1 values in the above three species encodings.

2.2.2 Normalizing Ordinal Observations

Ordinal observations are not necessarily numeric. However, they do have an implied ordering. For example, consider the levels of education progressed through by a student in the United States. One moves from preschool level to senior level before graduating. The levels have no true numerical value, but they do occur in a set order.

In order to normalize an ordinal set, one must preserve the order. One-of-n encoding loses the order. While the outputs are a vector, and it may appear that there is order, there is really no ordering, because most machine learning algorithms treat the individual outputs with no ordering at all. Just because output #1 and output #2 are next to each other, that does not mean they are in any way related. Implying such ordering might introduce bias.

To normalize ordinal observations, there two options. First, you can simply normalize with one-of-n encoding and forget the order. It could be that the order is not important, and in that case you can simply treat the observation as an unordered nominal data set. However, if you wish to preserve the order, you need to assign a whole number to each category, starting with zero. The number assignments for the grades would thus be as follows:

- Preschool (0)

- Kindergarten (1)

- First grade (2)

- Second grade (3)

- Third grade (4)

- Fourth grade (5)

- Fifth grade (6)

- Sixth grade (7)

- Seventh grade (8)

- Eighth grade (9)

- Freshman (10)

- Sophomore (11)

- Junior (12)

- Senior (13)

Now, we calculate a percent completion rate to determine the value for each level. There are fourteen total categories. So someone in sixth grade has completed 50% of their education.

```
7 / 14 = 0.5 (50%)
```

If we are normalizing between the range 0 to 1, then the percentage is sufficient at 0.5. However, if we are normalizing to the range -1 to 1, we need to apply the percent to that range. In order to do so, calculate the width of the range, which is the high value of the range subtracted by the low value.

```
width = (high − low) = (1 − (−1)) = 2
```

The percentage can be applied to the value of the width. If we are 50%, then we are halfway. Simply multiply the percent by the width.

```
widthDistance = width * 0.5 = 1
```

Now, add the width to the lower bound to get the normalized number. If we had achieved zero percent, we would be exactly at the lower bound (-1). If we had achieved one hundred percent, we would be exactly at the upper bound (+1). Sixth grade thus normalizes to 0.

```
lowerBound + widthDistance = −1 + 1 = 0
```

The above process can be summarized using Equation 2.1:

$$f(x) = \frac{(n_H - n_L)x}{N} + n_L \qquad (2.1)$$

The concept of calculating the width between the high and low values and taking the percent of that width to normalize the percentage is one that will be used again and again. The next two normalization techniques will build on that concept. For example, the next section shows how to reverse this process and denormalize a normalized ordinal observation.

2.2.3 Denormalizing Ordinal Observations

Denormalization is the opposite of normalization–it allows you to take a number that was normalized and convert it back to the original number. This is very useful when processing the output from a machine learning algorithm. For example, if you trained an algorithm to predict the grade level achievement of any given person, based on other observations, you would probably train the algorithm with current grade level observations that were normalized. Because the algorithm was trained with normalized data, it will also output normalized data. You need to denormalize this output so that it will have meaning in the context of the knowledge that you hoped to achieve.

I will now show you how to denormalize the grade level from the previous section, which is essentially the process of running the normalization steps in reverse. Let's say that the output is the normalized value of zero. To determine what grade that represents, we first need to calculate how far it is from the lower bound:

```
widthDistance = 0 - (-1) = 1
```

This converts our distance into the width. We can determine the percentage by calculating what percent into the width the above distance describes. We know the total width, because it is the range between the normalized upper and lower bounds (-1 and 1). In order to denormalize, you must know the range in which the data were originally normalized.

```
widthPercent = widthDistance / width = 1 / 2 = 0.5 (50%)
```

We now apply this 50% to our total number of categories, which, in this case, is 14.

```
categoryNumber = totalCategories * widthPercent = 14 * 0.5 = 7
```

The list giving value to the grades indicates that 7 corresponds to the sixth grade. We have thus denormalized the observation.

The above process can be summarized using Equation 2.2.

$$f(x) = \frac{N \cdot (x - n_L)}{n_H - n_L} \tag{2.2}$$

In the next section, we will see how to normalize quantitative observations.

2.2.4   Normalizing Quantitative Observations

Interval and ratio observations are normalized in the same way. We simply look at the range from which either of the quantitative observation types are drawn and normalize them to the desired range. The individual qualities that make an interval observation different from a ratio observation are meaningless for normalization.

Quantitative observations are always numeric, so they might not need to be normalized. While many machine-learning algorithms do require that numeric data be normalized to a specific range, some do not. It is important to know the numeric ranges required by the algorithm you are using in order to receive relevant output.

For practice, let's normalize the weight of an automobile. For the purposes of this example, I will estimate that the range for the weight of a car is between 100 and 4,000 kilograms. As mentioned in Chapter 1, the guessed low should be lower than the real low and the guessed high should be higher than the actual high. I would like to normalize this range between -1 and 1. The various highs and lows that apply to this scenario are listed as follows:

- dataHigh: The highest unnormalized observation.

- dataLow: The lowest unnormalized observation.

- normalizedHigh: The high end of the range to which the data will be normalized.

- normalizedLow: The low end of the range to which the data will be normalized.

Plugging in the values from above provides the following values:

- dataHigh: 4,000

- dataLow: 100

- normalizedHigh: 1

- normalizedLow: -1

We can now normalize the data. We need to calculate two ranges, or widths: **dataHigh** to **dataLow** and **normalizedHigh** to **normalizedLow**.

```
dataRange = dataHigh - dataLow = 4000 - 100 = 3900
normalizedRange = normalizedHigh - normalizedLow = 1 - (-1) = 2
```

Let's attempt to normalize a car weight of 1,000 kilograms. First, we need to determine how far into the **dataRange** this value is.

```
d = sample - dataLow = 1000 - 100 = 900
```

We now convert this to a percent.

```
dPct = d / dataRange = 900 / 3900 = 0.230769... (23%)
```

Rounded, this gives 0.23. We now calculate how far into the **normalizedRange** is 0.23.

```
dNorm = dRange * dPct = 2 * 0.23 = 0.46
```

We now add this to the normalized low, and we are done.

```
Normalized = normalizedLow + dNorm = -1 + 0.46 = -0.54
```

The normalized value is -0.54.

The above process can be summarized using Equation 2.3.

$$f(x) = \frac{(x - d_L)(n_H - n_L)}{(d_H - d_L)} + n_L \tag{2.3}$$

The next section will show how to reverse this process and denormalize a quantitative observation.

2.2.5   Denormalizing Quantitative Observations

To denormalize a quantitative observation, the normalization process is reversed. Let's use the normalized -0.54 from before. First, we calculate how far it is from the lower bound.

```
-0.54 - (-1) = 0.46
```

We now need to divide this number by the distance between the normalized min and max.

```
0.46 / 2 = 0.23
```

The result is 0.23, or 23%. Multiply this by **dataRange**.

```
0.23 * 3900 = 897
```

The value 897 is the distance into the **dataRange** that we are. To convert this to an actual weight, just add **dataLow**.

```
 897 + dataLow = 897 + 100 = 997
```

The value 997 is approximately equal to our original number of 1,000, so we have denormalized the weight. It is not exactly equal because I rounded on some of the divisions.

The above process can be summarized with Equation 2.4.

$$f(x) = \frac{(d_L - d_H)x - (n_H \cdot d_L) + d_H \cdot n_L}{(n_L - n_H)} \tag{2.4}$$

There are other ways to normalize both nominal and quantitative observations. These will be covered in the next section.

2.3 Other Methods of Normalization

There are many other means of normalizing observations. The means already presented are the most common. This section will introduce some other normalization methods for both quantitative and nominal observations.

2.3.1 Reciprocal Normalization

In this section we will look at a very simple means of normalization–reciprocal normalization. This normalization method supports both normalization and denormalization. However, reciprocal normalization is limited in that you cannot normalize into the range of your choice. Rather, reciprocal normalization always normalizes to a number in the range between -1 and 1.

Reciprocal normalization is very easy to implement. It requires no analysis of the data to determine high and low data values. Equation 2.5 shows how to use reciprocal normalization.

$$f(x) = \frac{1}{x} \qquad (2.5)$$

To see Equation 2.5 in use, consider normalizing the number five.

```
f(5.0) = 1.0/5.0 = 0.2
```

As you can see, the number five has been normalized to 0.2.

2.3.2 Reciprocal Denormalization

It is very easy to denormalize a number that has been normalized reciprocally. Because it is a reciprocal, it is the same equation.

$$f(x) = \frac{1}{x} \qquad (2.6)$$

To see Equation 2.6 in use, consider denormalizing the number 0.2.

```
f(0.2) = 1/(0.2) = 5.0
```

As you can see, we have easily completed a round trip. We normalized 5.0 to 0.2, and then denormalized 0.2 back to 5.0.

2.3.3 Understanding Equilateral Encoding

Equilateral encoding is a potential replacement for one-of-n encoding. I must admit that I am rather fond of this encoding method. If you've read my web-based articles, you will see that I use it often. Equilateral encoding brings two main features to the table.

- Requires one fewer output than one-of-n

- Spreads the "blame" better than one-of-n

Equilateral encoding uses one fewer output than one-of-n. This means that if you have ten categories to encode, one-of-n will require ten outputs while equilateral will require only nine. This gives you a slight performance boost.

The second feature is slightly more difficult to understand. Most training algorithms will score the output of a machine-learning algorithm based on the incorrectness of each output. Consider if you had 100 categories, which would require 100 outputs in one-of-n. The incorrectness will be centered primarily on two outputs. Recall that one-of-n specifies the selected category by which output has the highest value. The two outputs primarily involved in the incorrect answer are the output that mistakenly had the highest output and the output that should have had the correct output. All of the other outputs have an "ideal value" of either 0 or -1, depending on your normalization range.

This can cause a small problem for the one-of-n normalization method. If the algorithm had predicted a versicolor iris when it should have predicted a verginica iris, the actual output and ideal output would be as follows:

```
Ideal output:  -1, -1, 1
Actual output: -1, 1, -1
```

The problem is that only two of three actual outputs are incorrect. We would like to spread the "guilt" for this error over a larger percent of the actual outputs. This ensures that any training correct is applied equally to all outputs. To do this, a unique set of values for each class must be determined. Each set of values should have an equal Euclidean distance from the others. We will see more about Euclidean distance later in this chapter. The equal distance makes sure that incorrectly choosing Iris setosa for versicolor has the same error weight as choosing Iris setosa for Iris virginica.

Listing 2.1 shows the ideal classes normalized for one of n.

Listing 2.1: Calculated Class Equilateral Values 3 Classes

```
0:  -0.8660 ,  -0.5000
1:   0.8660 ,  -0.5000
2:   0.0000 ,   1.0000
```

Notice that there are two outputs for each of the three classes. This causes the decreased number of outputs provided by equilateral encoding relative to one-of-n encoding. Equilateral encoding always requires one fewer output than one-of-n encoding would have.

Look at the example concerning equilateral normalization. Just as before, consider whether the algorithm had predicted a versicolor iris when it should have predicted a verginica iris. The output and ideal are as follows:

```
Ideal output:  0.0000 ,  -1.0000
Actual output: -0.8660 ,  -0.5000
```

In this case, there are only two outputs, as is consistent with equilateral encoding. Now all outputs are producing incorrect values. Additionally, there are only two outputs to process, which slightly decreases the amount of data processed by the machine learning algorithm.

Algorithms will rarely give output that exactly matches any of their training values. To deal with this in one-of-n encoding, we simply look at what output was the highest. This method does not work for equilateral encoding. Equilateral encoding shows what calculated class equilateral value (Listing 2.1) has the shortest distance to the actual output of the algorithm.

What is meant by the assertion that each of the sets are equal in distance from each other? It means that their Euclidean distance is equal. Distances will be covered in greater detail in the next chapter. The Euclidean distance can be calculated using Equation 2.7.

$$\mathrm{d}(\mathbf{p}, \mathbf{q}) = \sqrt{\sum_{i=1}^{n}(p_i - q_i)^2} \tag{2.7}$$

In the above equation, the variable "q" represents the ideal output value; the variable "p" represents the actual output value. There are "n" sets of ideal and actual outputs. The next chapter will greatly expand upon Euclidean distance.

2.3.4 Implementing Equilateral Encoding

I will now show you the means by which the Euclidean encodings are calculated. I originally saw this algorithm in the book "Practical Neural Network Recipes in C++" by Masters (1993), who cited an article in PCAI as the actual source. (Guiver, 1991)

The equilateral algorithm can be a bit confusing, so I will demonstrate it in two different ways. First, I will demonstrate it graphically. We will normalize to the range -1 to 1. Consider if we were to simply encode two categories. Equilateral encoding requires one output less than the number of categories. For two categories, only one output is given. We can think of the single output as a single dimension. Figure 2.2 demonstrates what the one-dimensional output will look like.

Figure 2.2: Equilateral Encoding for Two Categories

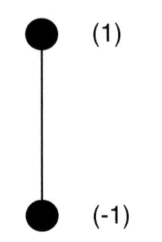

You can see the two points on the above line. We would have a single output of either 1 or -1.

If we had three categories, there would be two outputs. Think of this as two dimensions; it creates an equilateral triangle. This is where the name equilateral encoding comes from. Figure 2.3 shows how the three categories are encoded.

Figure 2.3: Equilateral Encoding for Three Categories

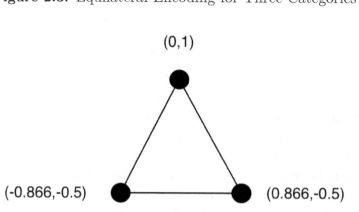

The key point of equilateral encoding is that each of these three categories must be equally distant from their neighbors. This allows the three categories to be represented in two dimensions. The dimensions that you see in the above figure match the encodings that we used in Figure 2.2.

We can also encode four categories. To encode four categories, we need three outputs, or three dimensions. This is depicted in in Figure 2.4.

Figure 2.4: Equilateral Encoding for Four Categories

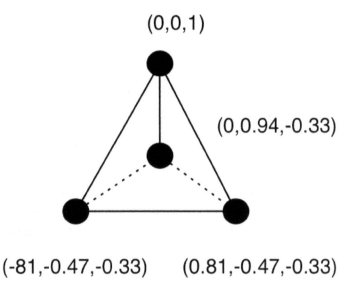

The above figure is a three-dimensional equilateral triangle. It is essentially a triangle-based pyramid. Just like all equilateral triangles, the lengths of all sides are equal.

We can also encode much larger numbers of categories. I cannot show these as dimensions because it is difficult to display a high dimensional figure in our three dimensional world, let alone on a two-dimensional book page.

Hopefully the graphical representations above show how the categories are arranged equidistantly from one another. Now I will show you how these numbers are actually calculated.

The equilateral encoding algorithm is usually implemented to output a matrix. The matrix is **N** by **N-1**, where **N** is the number of categories. Each row contains the encodings for one category. We will always create this matrix for normalization to the range -1 to 1. We will ultimately scale the completed matrix to whatever range we desire.

To begin creating this matrix we first seed the matrix for a two class encoding. As seen in Figure 2.1, this is simply the values -1 and 1. We begin by seeding these two values into the matrix.

```
result[0][0] = -1;
result[1][0] = 1;
```

We will now loop from two categories up to our **N** classes. We skip 1 because we already seeded for the case where we have one category only. We loop from 2 up to, but not including, **N**.

```
for k from 2 to N {
```

Next, we calculate a scaling factor. We will recursively build each successive matrix from the previous matrix. We seed for two categories, and then scale it to build the matrix for three categories. This is done with the following code:

```
f = sqrt( N * N - 1.0) / r;
```

Next, we loop over the portion of the matrix that we have already calculated and scale.

```
for i from 0 to k {
  for j from 0 to k-1 {
    result[i][j] *= f;
  }
}
```

We will now populate the edge of the matrix (columns) with the negative reciprocal of **N**.

```
r = -1 / N;
  for i from 0 to k {
    result[i][k - 1] = r;
}
```

Set the last value in the matrix to 1.0 and continue the previous "for loop."

```
result[k][k - 1] = 1.0;
}
```

Now that the loop is complete, we are ready to scale the matrix to the appropriate range. We use the same normalization formula shown in Equation 2.3.

We will use -1 and 1 for the low and high ranges for the data.

```
dataLow = -1;
dataHigh = 1;
```

We now loop over the entire matrix and scale it.

```
for row from 0 to N {
  for col from 0 to N-1 {
    result[row][col] = ((result[row][col] - dataLow)
    / (dataHigh - dataLow))
    * (normalizedHigh - normalizedLow) + normalizedLow;
  }
}
```

At this point, the matrix is now ready to be used as a table for equilateral encoding. If you wish to encode a category to equilateral, simply use the matrix as a lookup table and copy the row that corresponds to the category you are encoding. To decode, simply find the matrix row that has the lowest Euclidean distance to the output vector from your machine-learning algorithm.

2.4   Chapter Summary

This chapter described several normalization processes. Normalization is the process by which data is forced to conform to a specific range. The range is usually either -1 to +1 or 0 to 1. The range you choose is usually dependent on the machine-learning algorithm you are using. This chapter covered several different types of normalization.

Reciprocal normalization is a very simple normalization technique. This technique normalizes numbers to the range -1 to 1. Reciprocal normalization simply takes the reciprocal normalization and divides the number to normalize by 1.

Range normalization is more complex. However, range normalization allows you to normalize to any range you like. Additionally, range normalization must know the range of the input data. While this does allow you to make use of the entire normalization range, it also means that the entire data set must be analyzed ahead of time.

This chapter also showed how Euclidean distance can be used to determine how similar two vectors are to one another. The next chapter will expand upon the concept of distance and introduce additional distance metrics.

Chapter 3

Distance Metrics

- Vectors

- Euclidean Distance

- Manhattan Distance

- Chebyshev Distance

Distance is a very important measurement in both real life and Artificial Intelligence (AI). In real life, distance measures the degree of separation between two points. In AI, distance is used to calculate the similarity of two vectors. For AI, think of a vector as a one-dimensional array–the distance between two arrays is the similarity between them.

3.1 Understanding Vectors

A vector is essentially a one-dimension array. Do not confuse the dimensionality of the vector array with the dimensions of your problem. Even if your problem had 10 inputs, you would still have a vector. Vectors are always one dimension arrays. Your ten inputs would be stored in a vector of length ten.

In AI, a vector is usually used to store observations about a particular instance of something.

This maps to the real world concept of distance quite well. You can think of a point on a sheet of paper as having two dimensions, which are usually referred to as x and y. Likewise, a point in 3D space has three dimensions, usually labeled "**x**," "**y**," and "**z**." A two dimensional point can be stored in a vector of length two. Likewise, a 3D point can be stored in a vector of length three.

Our universe is made up of three perceivable dimensions, although sometimes "time" is treated as a fourth dimension. However, this is a manifold, and does not imply that time is a true dimension, at least in the sense of the first three. Because higher dimensions are imperceptible to humans, it is very difficult for us to comprehend dimensional spaces higher than three. Very high dimension spaces are very common in AI, however.

Recall from Chapter 2, "Normalizing Data," that the iris data set had the following five observations, or features:

- Sepal length

- Sepal width

- Petal length

- Petal width

- Iris species

You could think of this data set as a vector of length 5. However, the species feature must be handled differently than the other four. Vectors typically contain only numbers. The first four features are inherently numerical, but species is not. As demonstrated in chapter two, there are several ways to encode the species observation to additional dimensions.

Only simple numeric encoding translates the iris species to a single dimension. We must use additional dimensional encodings, such as one-of-n or equilateral, so that the species encodings are equidistant from each other. If we are classifying irises, we do not want our means of encoding to induce any biases.

Thinking of the iris features as dimensions in a higher dimensional space makes a great deal of sense. You can think of the individual samples (the rows in the iris data set) as points in this search space. Points closer together are likely to share similarities. Let's take a look at what this actually looks like by considering the following three rows from the iris data set:

```
5.1 ,3.5 ,1.4 ,0.2 , Iris −setosa
7.0 ,3.2 ,4.7 ,1.4 , Iris −versicolor
6.3 ,3.3 ,6.0 ,2.5 , Iris −virginica
```

If we use one-of-n encoding to the range 0 to 1, the above three rows would encode to the following three vectors:

```
[5.1 ,3.5 ,1.4 ,0.2 ,1 ,0 ,0]
[7.0 ,3.2 ,4.7 ,1.4 ,0 ,1 ,0]
[6.3 ,3.3 ,6.0 ,2.5 ,0 ,0 ,1]
```

Now that you have the data in vector form, you can calculate the distance between any two data items. The next few sections will describe several different methods to calculate the distance between two vectors.

3.2 Calculating Vector Distance

The distance between two vectors tells us the degree of similarity between two vectors. There are several different ways to calculate this vector distance.

3.2.1 Euclidean Distance

The Euclidean distance measurement is based off of the real, two-dimensional distance between two vectors. That is, it is the difference between the two points if you drew them on paper and measured with a ruler. This two-dimensional distance is based on the Pythagorean Theorem. Specifically, if you had two points **(x1,y1)** and **(x2,y2)**, the distance between the two would be described as follows:

$$d = \sqrt{(x_2 - x_1)^2 + (y_2 - y_1)^2} \qquad (3.1)$$

Figure 3.1 shows a two dimensional Euclidean distance between two points.

Figure 3.1: Two-Dimensional Euclidean Distance

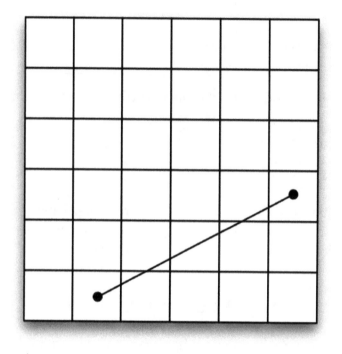

This would work fine for comparing two vectors of length two. However, most vectors are longer than two numbers. To calculate the Euclidean distance for any sized vector, use the general form of the Euclidean distance equation.

The Euclidean distance measurement is used often in Machine Learning. It is a quick way to compare two vectors of numbers that have the same number of elements. Consider three vectors, named vector **a**, vector **b**, and vector **c**. The Euclidean distance between array **a** and array **b** is 10. The Euclidean distance between array **a** and array **c** is 20. In this case, the contents of array **a** more closely match array **b** than they do array **c**.

Equation 3.1 shows the formula for calculating the Euclidean distance. (Deza, 2009)

$$d(\mathbf{p}, \mathbf{q}) = d(\mathbf{q}, \mathbf{p}) = \sqrt{\sum_{i=1}^{n}(q_i - p_i)^2} \tag{3.2}$$

The above equation shows us the Euclidean distance **d** between two arrays **p** and **q**. The above equation also states that **d(p,q)** is the same as **d(q,p)**. This simply means that the distance is the same no matter which end you start at. Calculation of the Euclidean distance is no more than summing the squares of the difference of each array element. Following this, the square root of this sum is taken. This square root is the Euclidean distance.

The following shows Equation 3.1 in pseudo code form.

```
function euclidean (position1, position2)
{
  sum = 0;
  for i from 0 to position1.length
  {
    d = position1[i] - position2[i];
    sum = sum + d * d;
  }

  return sqrt(sum);
}
```

3.2.2 Manhattan Distance

Manhattan distance is also commonly called taxicab distance. Euclidean distance can be thought of in terms of "as the crow flies." Manhattan distance calculates the distance as though you were driving on a city grid. (Krause, 2012) You can see two-dimensional Manhattan distance depicted in Figure 3.2.

Figure 3.2: Two-Dimension Manhattan Distance

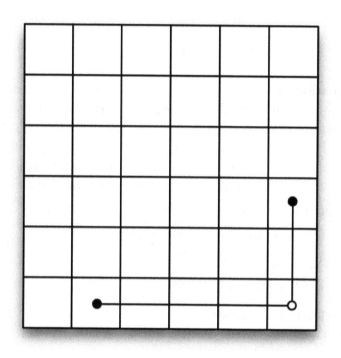

To calculate the Manhattan Distance between two points, add the absolute distances of each of the dimensions. Equation 3.2 performs this operation. (Deza, 2009)

$$d(\mathbf{p}, \mathbf{q}) = d(\mathbf{q}, \mathbf{p}) = \sum_{i=1}^{n} |p_i - q_i| \tag{3.3}$$

The primary difference between the Euclidean and Manhattan distances is that large distances are penalized disproportionately more than small distances in the Euclidean method. For example, when using Euclidean distance, the distance between two vectors that differ by one unit in two dimensions (the square root of two) is less than the distance between two vectors that differ by two units in only one dimension (two), whereas they would both be equal (two) using Manhattan distance.

The following shows Equation 3.2 in pseudo code form.

```
function manhattan (position1, position2)
{
  sum = 0;
  for i from 0 to position1.length
  {
    d = abs(position1[i] - position2[i]);
    sum = sum + d;
  }

  return sum;
}
```

3.2.3 Chebyshev Distance

The Chebyshev distance is also commonly called the chessboard distance. If you've ever played chess, you can think of it as the number of moves that a king would take to move between the two points. Figure 3.3 shows how far each of the locations is from the first point.

Figure 3.3: Two-Dimension Chebyshev Distance

4	4	4	4	4	4
3	3	3	3	3	3
2	2	2	2	2	3
2	1	1	1	2	3
2	1	●	1	2	3
2	1	1	1	2	3

To calculate the Chebyshev distances, take the maximum of the dimension differences. This is described in Equation 3.3. (Deza, 2009)

$$d(\mathbf{p}, \mathbf{q}) = d(\mathbf{q}, \mathbf{p}) = \max_i(|p_i - q_i|) \tag{3.4}$$

The Chebyshev distance can be useful when you want to focus on the dimension with the largest distance. When all dimensions are either normalized or in approximately the same range and the worst dimension governs the similarity between the two vectors, the Chebyshev distance is best to use.

The following shows Equation 3.3 in pseudo code form.

```
function chebyshev (position1, position2)
{
  result = 0;
  for i from 0 to position1.length
  {
    d = abs(position1[i] - position2[i]);
    result = max(result, d);
  }

  return result;
}
```

3.3   Optical Character Recognition

OCR is a very common example of machine learning. You've probably seen it on the Internet. Most of these examples are of the same form. You draw a series of characters and a very complex machine-learning algorithm (often a neural network) learns your characters and can recognize new ones.

Euclidean distance can be used to perform basic Optical Character Recognition (OCR). The program allows you to draw individual characters and add them to a list of known characters. The characters you draw are images, which are a popular source of input for AI. This section describes how to normalize an image using down sampling. There are more advanced methods than this, but down sampling is often effective. (Lyons, 2009)

The first step is to take a raw image that you want the program to recognize. A real OCR package would have to process the image and determine its individual characters. For this example, we will simplify the process by only using a single character. Figure 3.4 shows such an image–a zero digit.

Figure 3.4: Drawing a Zero

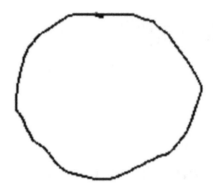

You may have noticed there is quite a bit of extra space at the sides of the digit I drew. This could present a problem. The machine learning algorithm will be looking at a grid of pixels as inputs. What if the user draws the zero in the upper left corner during training, but in the lower-right corner when actually using the algorithm? The algorithm would be unlikely to recognize the second drawing, because the pixels would be on different inputs. Because of this, it is necessary to crop. To crop, just drop lines from the top, left, right, and bottom until they touch a pixel. Figure 3.5 shows the cropping lines.

Figure 3.5: Cropping the Digit

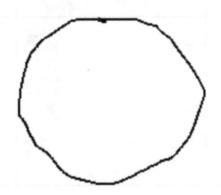

Then crop the image. While doing so, we will also down sample. This will cause us to have fewer pixels to review and resolves issues related to size. If the user draws the digit at different sizes, down sampling will eliminate the possibility that the sizing will affect the program's reading.

Why do we need to decrease the number of pixels? Consider a full-color image that is 300x300 pixels. We would have 90,000 pixels times the three RGB colors, giving 270,000 total pixels. If we had an input for each pixel, that would be 270,000 inputs. Each image is a vector, and a 270k-dimension vector would be very large! To make the program more robust, it is necessary to decrease the number of inputs.

Figure 3.6 shows what the image looks like down sampled to 7x5 pixels.

Figure 3.6: Down Sampling

To perform the down sample, lay a 7x5 grid over the high-resolution image. For each grid cell, make the entire cell black, if even one underlying pixel is black.

Because we have a 7x5 grid, we now can create a vector of size 7x5 or 35 inputs. We create a vector for each digit and store its cropped, down sampled form in a table. When the user draws new characters to recognize, we will crop and down sample. A new vector is created for each image. We then find the digit in our table with the least distance from our new image. We determine the new image to be the same digit as the digit in the table with the lowest distance.

3.4   Chapter Summary

Vectors are a very important component of machine learning. Both input and output are in the form of vectors in the context of a machine learning algorithm. The memory of the machine learning algorithm is typically thought of as a vector. Vectors can also be considered as coordinates in an n-dimensional space. This allows us to compare the similarity of two vectors by computing the distance between them.

There are many different ways to calculate the distance between two vectors. One of the most basic is Euclidean distance. Euclidean distance uses the regular distance formula between two-dimensional points. This same formula can be applied to any number of dimensions. Manhattan distance and Chebyshev distance may also be used.

Optical Character Recognition (OCR) can be implemented through simple distance calculation. We begin by creating a table of known characters and a table of vectors to represent these characters. These vectors are created by cropping and down sampling the character images. New images are cropped and down sampled, as well. We then determine the new character to be the character that has the least distance from one of the vectors stored in the table.

Random numbers are a very important concept to machine learning. We will often use a random vector as the initial state of a machine learning algorithm. This initial random state is then refined during training. Random numbers can also be used for Monte Carlo techniques for training. The next chapter will cover random numbers.

Chapter 4

Random Number Generation

- Pseudorandom Number Generation

- Linear Congruential Generator (LCG)

- Multiply With Carry (MWC)

- Mersenne Twister

- Monte Carlo Method

Random numbers are very important to many machine learning algorithms and training techniques. When performed by computers, random number generation is called pseudorandom number generation (PRNG). The prefix "pseudo" means that something is implied, rather than defined. This is the case with computer generated random numbers, as a computer is a completely logical machine that follows instructions and can only simulate randomization. Given exactly the same inputs and internal state, a computer will always produce exactly the same outputs. (Turing, 1948)

Despite these logical limitations to randomization, computers can be very effective at pseudorandom number generation. Two criteria are often used to judge the effectiveness of a PRNG: the randomness of the algorithm and the security of the PRNG algorithm. An algorithm can be very random, but is not necessarily cryptographically secure. For AI, we care primarily about the randomness of an algorithm. Security is more important for an encryption algorithm. A secure PRNG is called a Cryptographically Secure Pseudorandom Number Generator (CSPRNG).

Good randomness is defined by whether a PRNG's period produces detectable repeating sequences within a period and how long the PRNG's periods are. In this context, a period is the amount of random numbers that a PRNG can produce before it begins to repeat the sequence. Each period is essentially a string of numbers, and each PRNG compiles a series of identical periods. The larger the period, the more random a generator is. The fewer repeating sequences evident inside of a period there are, the more random a generator is.

It is important to understand the distinction between regular PRNGs and CSPRNGs. All PRNGs and CSPRNGs have an internal state. If you know the internal state of the generator, you will know what the next random number will be. PRNGs and CSPRNGs can both potentially produce high quality random number sequences. The primary difference between PRNGs and CSPRNGs is that you can typically determine a PRNG's internal state by analyzing the numbers. However, you cannot determine a CSPRNG's internal state in a reasonable amount of time. This distinction is critical for cryptology, but is not as important for AI. In AI, the quality of the numbers is most important, while the numbers' likelihood of providing information about the algorithm's internal state is of less importance.

4.1   PRNG Concepts

There are several important concepts that nearly all PRNGs share. These define how the PRNG performs and what its expected output can be. Common concepts that all PRNGs share include the following:

- Seed

- Internal State

- Period

The seed defines the sequence of random numbers you will get, as well as the initial internal state. You should always get the same sequence of random numbers for the same given seed, and nearly every seed should produce a different sequence of random numbers.

The internal state comprises the variables that the PRGN uses to produce both the random numbers and the next internal state. If you know the internal state and the type of PRGN or CSPRNG algorithm, you can predict the next random number.

The length of each random number sequence is the period. Once the period is up, the random PRGN will repeat. That is why the PRGN is considered a periodic function–because it repeats its values at regular intervals or periods. Figure 4.1 shows the sine function, which is perhaps the most well-known periodic function.

Figure 4.1: The Sine Function is Periodic

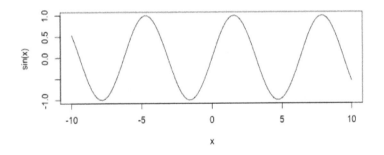

As you can see from the above figure, the sine function has a period of 2*PI, or approximately 6.28.

4.2   Random Distribution Types

You will usually want your random numbers to be uniformly distributed. PRNGs typically provide a random number between 0 and 1, with equal probability of getting any particular number in that range. You can see the results of generating a large number of random numbers between 0 and 1 in Figure 4.2, which shows a uniform distribution of random numbers.

Figure 4.2: Uniform Distribution of Random Numbers

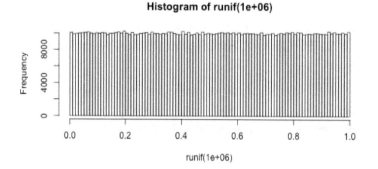

As you can see from figure 4.2 above, the random numbers are evenly distributed between 0 and 1. This is called a uniform distribution, or a uniform random number. It provides equal probability of getting any option within the specified range.

Most programming languages provide a means to generate uniformly distributed random numbers between 0 and 1. You can scale this random number out to whatever range you desire. This works very similarly to normalization. If the function **rand()** returns a random number between 0 and 1, then equation 4.1 scales it to a range between **high** and **low**.

$$rnd(low, high) = rnd() \cdot (high - low) + low \qquad (4.1)$$

The above equation allows you to generate a random number in any range.

Some programming languages also provide a means to generate a normally distributed random number. Figure 4.3 shows such normally distributed random numbers.

Figure 4.3: Normal Distribution of Random Numbers

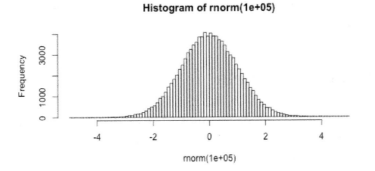

The random numbers with the greatest probability are clustered around 0. There is really no defined upper and lower bound. Each whole number represents a standard deviation. As the standard deviations increase on both the positive and negative sides, the probability of getting a random number decreases greatly. Beyond 4 or -4, it is very rare to get a number. Normally distributed random numbers are often useful when you want to vary a number by a small random amount.

Not all programming languages support normally distributed random numbers, however. The functions that support these PRNGs are listed here.

```
C#
    Uniform: Random.NextDouble
    Normal: NA
C/C++
    Uniform: rand
    Normal: NA
Java
    Uniform: Random.NextDouble
    Normal: Random.nextGaussian
Python
    Uniform: random.random
    Normal: random.randn
R
    Uniform: runif
    Normal: rnorm
```

If your language does not support normal distributions, you can use the Box Muller transformation to transform uniformly distributed random numbers into normally distributed random numbers. Box Muller is discussed at length later in this chapter.

4.3   Roulette Wheels

Another popular random number technique is called the roulette wheel (Back, 1996). This technique only bears a slight resemblance to an actual roulette wheel, as seen in a casino. Roulette wheels are useful when you would like to choose between three or more categories. For example, consider if you wanted to create a robot to randomly explore a grid and your robot can perform only the following three actions:

- Move forward

- Turn left

- Turn right

Although the robot moves randomly, you might not want an even distribution among these three directions. You might want the robot to move as follows:

- Move forward (80% of the time)

- Turn left (10% of the time)

- Turn right (10% of the time)

Such a random number generation is relatively easy to implement. You must order these choices so that they each share part of the 0 to 1 range that a uniform PRNG will generate numbers for.

If **x** is the random number, then the following list defines our actions.

```
if 0<x<0.8 then move forward
if 0.8<x<0.9 then turn left
if 0.9<x<1.0 then turn right
```

The first line is needed because x will be below 0.8 in 80% of the cases. The second line is needed because x will be between 0.8 and 0.9 in 10% of the cases. Likewise, x will be between 0.9 and 1.0 in 10% of the cases.

4.4 PRNG Algorithms

There are many different PRNG algorithms. Often, there is a tradeoff between execution speed and randomness. Some algorithms are simply better than others. In this section, we will review some of the PRNG algorithms. Finally, we will review the Box Muller transformation. Box Muller is not a PRNG algorithm, but it can take the output of a uniform PRNG algorithm and produce normally distributed random numbers.

Performance is another very important consideration for PRNG selection. Most AI algorithms require a very large quantity of random numbers. Random number generation can thus be a very important consideration that affects the overall efficiency of the algorithm.

It is not critical that you understand how all of the PRNG algorithms function internally. You can make use of the random numbers generated by an algorithm without learning the algorithm's internal details.

The PRNG algorithms covered in this book are as follows:

- Linear Congruential Generator (LCG)

- Multiply With Carry (MWC)

- Mersenne Twister

Different programming languages will use different PRNG algorithms. If your programming language does not use the algorithm you desire, the algorithm can be implemented separately in that language.

4.4.1 Linear Congruential Generator

The Linear Congruential Generator (LCG) is one of the oldest and most common PRNG algorithms in use. LCG is the built-in PRNG for C/C++, Java, and C#. LCG is documented in Donald Knuth's The Art of Programming, Section 3.2.1. (Knuth, 1997). LCGs should not be used for applications where high quality randomness is needed. LCG is not typically useful for a Monte Carlo simulation because of the serial correlation. Serial correlation is the relation of a variable to itself over time. This means LCG random numbers are not high quality, nor are they suitable for cryptographic applications.

LCG is straightforward to implement and understand. It is implemented through a linear function clipped into a defined period. The equation for LCG is shown in Equation 4.2.

$$X_{n+1} = (aX_n + c) \qquad (\mathrm{mod}\ m) \tag{4.2}$$

The variables and acceptable ranges for the above equation are defined as follows:

```
m,  0 < m,  The modulus
a,  0 < a < m,  The multiplier
c,  0 <= c < m,  The increment
X0,  0 <= X0 < m,  The seed, or starting value
```

The **seed** value is updated with each random number generated. For LCG, the next seed is the internal state. These random numbers will be integers. They can be converted into the 0 to 1 range by dividing the random numbers by the maximum integer that the algorithm can produce. The maximum integer produced will depend on the settings of **m**, **a**, and **c**.

The values chosen for **m**, **a**, and **c** will have a great impact on the randomness of the numbers generated by the PRNG. Typically, you should not choose values of your own for **m**, **a**, and **c**. Much research has gone into finding optimal values. Wikipedia has a very good summary of the values used by various PRNGs.

http://en.wikipedia.org/wiki/Linear_congruential_generator

I typically use the values used by the GCC compiler.

```
m = 2e31
a = 1103515245
c = 12345
```

While LCG is a very commonly used PRNG, the Mersenne Twister is often a better alternative.

4.4.2 Multiply with Carry

The Multiply with Carry (MWC) PRNG was invented by George Marsaglia for the purpose of generating sequences of random integers with large periods. (Marsaglia, 1991) It uses an initial seed set from two to many thousands of randomly chosen values. The main advantages of the MWC method are that it invokes simple computer integer arithmetic and leads to very fast generation of sequences of random numbers. MWC has immense periods, ranging from around 260 to 2 to the power of 2000000.

MWC works somewhat similarly to LCG. Assuming 32 bit registers, LCG uses only the lower 32 bits of the multiplication (Equation 4.2). MWC makes use of these higher bits through a carry. Additionally, multiple seed values are used. These seed values are typically created with another PRNG algorithm, such as LCG.

We must first define a variable **r** to describe the "lag" of the MWC. We must provide a number of seed values equal to **r**. Like the LCG algorithm (Equation 4.2), we also have a modulus and a multiplier. However, there is no increment in this case. The equation used to generate the random integers for MWC is shown in Equation 4.3.

$$x_n = (ax_{n-r} + c_{n-1}) \bmod b, \; n \geq r \tag{4.3}$$

The multiplier is represented by **a**, while the modulus is represented by **b**. There is an additional variable **c**, which represents the carry. The calculation for the carry is shown in Equation 4.4.

$$c_n = \left\lfloor \frac{ax_{n-r} + c_{n-1}}{b} \right\rfloor, \; n \geq r \tag{4.4}$$

The variable **n** represents the number in the sequence you are calculating. It is important that **n** always be greater than **r**. This is because the **x** values before **n** are the seed values, and we have **r** seeds.

Equation 4.4 is very similar to 4.3, but while 4.3 uses the modulus operator to return the remainder, 4.4 actually carries out the division. We then use the floor of this result as the carry. The floor is the largest integer part of a number. For example, the floor of 7.3 would be 7. However, the floor of -7.3 would be -8. The floor of -7 would be -7.

The reason that we use the **floor** operator in Equation 4.4 is to ensure an integer result. Typically these operations are carried out on integer variables so the floor operator is given to make Equation 4.4 mathematically correct. The code examples for MWC do not make use of a call to the **floor** function.

The MWC generator has a much larger period than LCG, and its implementations are typically very fast to execute. It is an improvement over LCG, but it is not a commonly used generator. It is not the default random number generator for any computer language that I am aware of.

4.4.3   Mersenne Twister

The Mersenne Twister is a PRNG developed in 1997 by Makoto Matsumoto and Takuji Nishimura. It provides for fast generation of very high quality pseudorandom integers. The Mersenne Twister was designed specifically to address many of the flaws found in older algorithms. (Matsumoto, 1998)

The Mersenne Twister is a very popular PRNG. It is the "built in" PRNG for Ruby, Python, and R. This book's examples also contain implementations for other languages. The Mersenne Twister algorithm creates high quality random numbers suitable for Monte Carlo simulations. Mersenne Twister is not a cryptographically secure generator. However, its execution speed and high quality randomness make it a very attractive generator for AI.

The name Mersenne Twister comes from the fact that that the period of the Mersenne Twister is always chosen to be a Mersenne prime number.

A prime number is any number that can only be divided evenly by itself and one. For example, 5 is a prime number. A Mersenne prime number is any number **n** where **M** is also a prime number, as seen in Equation 4.5.

$$M_n = 2^n - 1 \tag{4.5}$$

To see how this works, consider 5, which is a Mersenne prime number.

```
2^5 = 32
32 - 1 = 31
```

The number 31 is prime, so the number 5 is a Mersenne prime number. You can find a list of the known Mersenne prime numbers at the following URL.

http://en.wikipedia.org/wiki/Mersenne_prime

Some other Mersenne primes are shown below.

```
2
3
5
7
13
17
19
31
61
89
107
127
521
607
1,279
2,203
2,281
3,217
4,253
4,423  (Wikipedia, 2013)
```

The Mersenne Twister algorithm's implementation is much more complex than the algorithms already described in this chapter, and a full description of it is beyond the scope of this book. The code examples do contain an implementation of the Mersenne Twister based on the original C implementation provided by Matsumoto.

One of the more tricky aspects of implementing the Mersenne Twister is that it relies on bit shifts. This can be tricky for languages that do not support unsigned numbers. Java's non-support of unsigned numbers makes a Java implementation particularly tricky. For other languages, it is important to make sure that the variable sizes match the original C code.

4.4.4 Box Muller Transformation

Not all programming languages support the generation of random numbers in a normal distribution. You might also be using a custom PRNG not provided by your programming language. There is an algorithm that can transform a continuous random number distribution into a normal one. This algorithm is called the Box Muller Transformation. (Box, 1958)

The following pseudo code can be used to transform regular continuous random numbers into normal random numbers. (Ross, 2009) The Box Muller Transformation generates numbers two at a time. To keep track of the pairs, we will place the two numbers into **y1** and **y2**. We will use the variable **useLast** to track if there is a value in **y2** waiting to be used. The variable **y1** will ultimately be returned, so if **useLast** is set to true, then move **y2** into **y1**.

```
if (useLast)
{
  y1 = y2;
  useLast = false;
} else
{
```

Begin by generating **x1** and **y1**, both in the range -1 to 1. Because **rand()** normally returns 0 to 1, we scale **x1** and **y1**. We then square and sum both **x1** and **y1**, giving **w**. We continue until we have a **w** that is greater than or equal to 1.0.

```
do
{
  x1 = 2.0 * rand() - 1.0;
  x2 = 2.0 * rand() - 1.0;
  w = x1 * x1 + x2 * x2;
} while (w >= 1.0);
w= sqrt((-2.0 * log(w)) / w);
```

Box Muller works by calculating two independent uniform distributions, stored in **x1** and **x2**. A scaling factor **w** is calculated across them; it allows **x1** and **x2** to be converted into a normally distributed random number.

```
  y1 = x1 * w;
  y2 = x2 * w;
  useLast = true;
}
```

We scale both **x1** and **x2**, storing the results in **y1** and **y2**.

```
return Y1;
```

We immediately return **y1** and set **useLast** to **true**. The next call to the function will return **y2**.

4.5 Estimating PI with Monte Carlo

Monte Carlo algorithms attempt to estimate through random sampling, as it can be time intensive to calculate the actual value. Monte Carlo makes use of random samples to generate a good estimate. There are many different Monte Carlo techniques, some of which are hybrids between Monte Carlo and other techniques. (Robert, 2005) Later in this book, we will learn a Monte Carlo method called Simulated Annealing.

One simple example of Monte Carlo is its estimation of the value of PI. Figure 4.4 shows a circle perfectly inscribed inside of a square.

Figure 4.4: A Circle Inscribed in a Square

We will now place random points inside of the square and circle. The ratio of points inside to outside will tell us the value of PI. The area of the square is its length multiplied by its width. Because a square has the same width as length, the area of the square is essentially the width times itself, or width squared.

A circle's area is PI times its radius squared. The diameter of the circle is the same as the width of the square. We will calculate the ratio of the area of the circle to the square by using Equation 4.6.

$$p = \frac{\pi r^2}{(2r)^2} = \frac{\pi}{4} \tag{4.6}$$

The width of the square is the same as two times the circle's radius. So we can describe the square's diameter as two times the radius squared. We will take the ratio of points inside the circle to outside and multiply by 4. This will give us an approximation of PI.

The pseudo code to produce this is shown below.

```
tries = 0;
success = 0;
for i from 0 to 10000
{
 // pick a point at random.
 x = rand();
 y = rand();
 tries = ties + 1;
 // was the point inside of a circle?
 if (x * x + y * y <= 1)
 {
 success++;
 }
}
pi = 4 * success / tries;
```

As we consider more points we gain a more accurate approximation of PI.

4.6   Chapter Summary

Random numbers are very useful to AI programs, particularly Monte Carlo simulations. A number of different random number generation algorithms exist. All are called pseudorandom number generators (PRNG). These random number generators vary in their ability to produce quality random numbers.

Some PRNGs are said to be cryptographically secure (CSPRNG). A random number generator may produce high quality random numbers, yet not be cryptographically secure. CSPRNG implies that the internal state of the algorithm cannot easily be guessed by observing the output of the algorithm. It is not necessary to have a CSPRNG for AI applications. For AI, we are primarily interested in obtaining high quality random numbers and less interested in ensuring that these numbers do not reveal the internal state of the algorithm.

One of the earliest and most common PRNG algorithms is the Linear Congruential Generator (LCG). While LCG can produce decent random numbers, the quality is not good enough for Monte Carlo simulations. Multiply with Carry (MWC) was created to overcome some of the limitations of LCG. The Mersenne Twister algorithm quickly produces high quality random numbers. Mersenne Twister is acceptable for a Monte Carlo simulation.

A Monte Carlo simulation estimates a large problem by sampling small pieces of it. In this chapter, we saw that we could estimate PI using Monte Carlo. We looked at a circle that was perfectly inscribed inside of a square. We randomly chose points and determined what points were inside of the circle and what were not. The ratio of these two point sets told us the value of PI.

The last two chapters introduced distance calculation and random numbers. The next chapter will show us an algorithm that combines both techniques. It will show how observations can be divided into similar groups based on their distances from each other. K-Means clustering is one common technique for performing such divisions.

Chapter 5

K-Means Clustering

- Clustering

- Centroid

- Unsupervised Training

- K-Means

In previous chapters we saw that the input to a machine-learning algorithm is typically a vector of floating point numbers. Each of these vectors is called an observation, while the individual numbers that make up the vectors are called features.

In this chapter we will learn about clustering. Clustering is the process of placing together observations with similar features, and thereby creating a cluster.

Clustering is a very useful means of breaking observations into a specified number of groups. Most clustering algorithms require you to specify the number of groups beforehand. Some clustering algorithms can automatically determine an optimal number of groups. This chapter focuses on the K-Means algorithm.

The process of clustering a finite number of observations into a specified number of clusters is called NP-Hard. NP-Hard is an abbreviation for non-deterministic polynomial-time. Informally, NP-Hard can be defined as problems that cannot be solved via a brute force search, when there are simply too many different combinations to search every potential solution to a problem. Clustering a non-trivial number of observations is NP-Hard.

K-Means makes use of random numbers to search for an acceptable clustering arrangement for the observations. Because the algorithm is based on random numbers, K-Means is said to be nondeterministic. This means that multiple runs of the K-Means algorithm will result in different assignment of observations to clusters.

The opposite of a nondeterministic algorithm is a deterministic algorithm. Deterministic algorithms always produce the same output, given consistent input. Nearly all of the algorithms presented in this book are nondeterministic.

Clustering can be used both independently and as a component to a larger machine-learning algorithm. Independently, clustering can be used to place similar items into groups. For example, you may have a large amount of observations that represent the buying habits of individuals. If each observation represents a customer, customers can be clustered. This allows you to make suggestive sales to customers based on what other customers in the same cluster have purchased.

Genetic algorithms that use speciation often make use of clustering as a component of the genetic algorithm. Genetic algorithms find solutions following a process that is loosely modeled after Darwinian evolution. (Banzhaf, 1998) Potential solutions to a problem compete with each other and reproduce to create potentially better solutions that carry the desirable traits from the parents. Often it is desirable to break the potential solutions into species and only allow breeding within a species. Because the potential solutions are often vectors, K-Means can be used to speciate the potential solutions. (Green, 2009)

The K-Means algorithm has been around, in various forms, since the 1950s. This algorithm has gone through a number of revisions by various researchers. James MacQueen first used the term "K-Means" in 1967. The actual idea for K-Means goes back to Hugo Steinhaus in 1957. Stuart Lloyd first proposed the standard algorithm in 1957 at Bell labs. However, his work wasn't published outside Bell labs until 1982. In 1965, E. W. Forgy published essentially the same method, which is why it is sometimes referred to as the Lloyd-Forgy algorithm. A more efficient version was proposed and published in Fortran by Hartigan and Wong in 1975 and revised in 1979.

5.1 Understanding Training Sets

Sets of observations are usually grouped into large collections called training sets. This data is used to train the machine-learning algorithm. Training is the process where the machine-learning algorithm is modified so that the output from the algorithm provides the desired information.

There are two very broad classes of machine learning algorithm that take very different types of training sets. Training is either supervised or unsupervised. When performing unsupervised training, you provide the algorithm with an input observation as a vector. However, you do not specify an output vector that represents the expected, or ideal, output. Clustering is a type of unsupervised training.

5.1.1 Unsupervised Training

Recall the iris data set used in previous chapters? The iris data set has been applied to many different machine-learning algorithms. It can be used for both supervised and unsupervised training. This section shows how the iris data set can be applied to both.

First, we will take a look at how we would present the iris data set for unsupervised clustering. Recall that the iris data set consists of four individual ratio observations about the dimensions of the iris petals. Additionally, the species of the iris is specified. Listing 5.1 shows a sampling from the iris data set.

Listing 5.1: Several Rows from the Iris Data Set

```
5.1 ,3.5 ,1.4 ,0.2 , Iris −setosa
4.9 ,3.0 ,1.4 ,0.2 , Iris −setosa
...
7.0 ,3.2 ,4.7 ,1.4 , Iris −versicolor
6.4 ,3.2 ,4.5 ,1.5 , Iris −versicolor
...
6.3 ,3.3 ,6.0 ,2.5 , Iris −virginica
5.8 ,2.7 ,5.1 ,1.9 , Iris −virginica
```

For an unsupervised clustering, we would most likely use the first four measurements and ignore the species. We might tag the observations to the species, perhaps for later comparison. However, the clustering algorithm does not need to know the species, because this is unsupervised training. The algorithm will not aim to determine what species the iris is, but will rather place the observations into clusters based on similarities among the observations.

It is also important to note that it is not necessary to normalize the four observations. K-Means clustering does not inherently require normalization. Some other algorithms will require normalization, of course. For clustering the iris data set, normalization is optional. You should only use normalization with K-Means if one or more of the features are so large that it might overwhelm the others. The four ratio features of the iris data set are all reasonably close in value, so normalization is not necessary in this case.

The iris data set does not have enough information expressed in the four ratio features to properly cluster it by species. This is okay. For clustering, we are really trying to visualize how close observations are and what clusters they might fall into.

Figure 5.1 shows one attempt to cluster the iris data set.

Figure 5.1: Iris Data Set Clustered

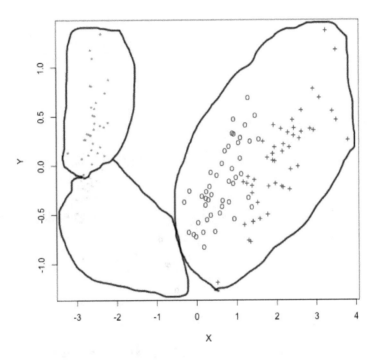

It will take some explanation to show what Figure 5.1 depicts, as there is quite a bit going on in this graph. The clusters are shown by color. They are also circled, for the benefit of those viewing this in black and white media. You can see that there are three clusters: red, green, and blue.

Each point is designated one of three total characters, which are pluses, asterisks, and O's. The character type indicates the species, as specified by the file in Listing 5.1. If the clustering algorithm were able to correctly cluster the iris species, each character of the same type would be the same color. If you look at Figure 5.1, you will see that this is not the case.

While you can see that the clusters are clearly defined, they do not line up with the species. This is mostly unavoidable. K-Means will sometimes come closer to picking the species, due to its random nature. However, if you look at Figure 5.1, you will see that two regions are linearly separable. This means you could draw a line between them. However, two of the iris species are not linearly separable. There is overlap. It would be impossible for unsupervised clustering alone to find the separation between these two species.

You may be wondering how the four dimensional iris vectors were drawn on a two dimensional graph. I used R to reduce the dimensions to two for graphing purposes. Dimension reduction is a common technique for data visualization, and was done using R's **cmdscale** function.

5.1.2   Supervised Training

Supervised training is more restricted than unsupervised. A supervised training set consists of pairs of input and ideal output data. For the iris data set, you would input the four ratio measurement observations as a four dimension input vector. You would likely use one-of-n encoding to encode the species data into an ideal output vector. The machine-learning algorithm would be rated on how well it produced the expected output vector, given the input vector. We will use supervised training with the iris data later in this book.

5.2   Understanding the K-Means Algorithm

The K-Means algorithm is relatively simple to implement. It works by assigning observations into a set number of clusters. There are three distinct steps to the K-Means algorithm: (Russel, 2009)

- Initialization Step

- Assignment Step

- Update Step

There are two different means by which the initialization step can be accomplished. (Hamerly, 2002) These two initialization methods will be covered after we cover the other two steps. For now, just assume that the observations are initially assigned to the clusters by some means.

5.2.1 Assignment Step

The assignment and update steps are repeated until no observation moves to a new cluster. Each cluster is defined by two aspects. The first is its centroid, which is a vector of the same length as the observation. It is essentially an observation itself, but in fact represents the average of all observations inside the cluster. The centroid is thus essentially the point that is at the center of all observations in a cluster. In addition to a centroid, each cluster holds a list of observations assigned to that cluster.

The assignment step loops over all of the observations and assigns them to the cluster that has the nearest centroid. By nearest, I mean the shortest distance between the two vectors. Typically, the Euclidean distance is used; however, any of the distance algorithms from the last chapter would work.

It is also important for the update step to keep track of whether any observation moves from one cluster to another. This allows the K-Means algorithm to know when the algorithm is complete. If no observations move to a new cluster, then the K-Means algorithm is considered complete.

The pseudo code for the assignment step is shown here. First, we set a variable named **done** to **true**. We start out assuming that we are done. If any observation is reassigned from one cluster to another, we will set **done** to **false**.

```
done = true
```

We must now check each cluster and determine whether any of that cluster's observations might need to be moved to another cluster. We do not keep a list of observations; the observations "live" inside of clusters.

```
foreach (cluster in clusters)
{
```

We now loop over every observation in the current cluster and reassign if necessary.

```
foreach(observation in cluster)
{
```

Find what cluster is currently closest to the observation. The **findNearest-Cluster** function simply finds the minimum Euclidean distance between the current observation and the centroids of all the clusters.

```
targetCluster = findNearestCluster(observation);
```

If the **targetCluster** is not the current cluster, then a move must occur. Perform the move and record that we are not done by setting **done** to **false**.

```
    if (targetCluster != cluster)
    {
      cluster.remove(observation);
      targetCluster.add(observation);
      done = false;
    }
  }
}
return done;
```

Finally, return the value of done so that the rest of the program can decide if it should continue iterating or exit.

5.2.2   Update Step

The update step is executed after the assignment step. These two steps keep cycling until there no observations change clusters during the assignment step. Like many machine learning algorithms, K-Means is iterative. The training process goes through a large number of iterations, and every iteration should see some gradual improvement. At some point, each iteration brings little or no improvement. This is when an iterative algorithm stops.

The real work of the update step is to recalculate the centroids for each of the clusters. During the previous assignment step, it is likely that the contents of each cluster were changed. Because of this, the centroid for each cluster may have become invalid. To account for this, we need to recalculate each cluster's centroid, which is a matter of simply calculating the mean of each feature of the observation. For example, if the following three iris flowers were all in a cluster, we would need to calculate a mean vector of four dimensions. This mean becomes the centroid for the cluster.

```
5.1,3.5,1.4,0.2,Iris−setosa
4.9,3.0,1.4,0.2,Iris−setosa
7.0,3.2,4.7,1.4,Iris−versicolor
```

This vector would be calculated as follows:

```
element1 = (5.1 + 4.9 + 7.0) / 3 = 5.7
element2 = (3.5 + 3.0 + 3.2) / 3 = 3.2
element3 = (1.4 + 1.4 + 4.7) / 3 = 2.5
element4 = (0.2 + 0.2 + 1.4) /3 = 0.6
```

Which results in the following centroid:

```
[5.7,  3.2,  2.5,  0.6]
```

Of course, as discussed previously, the iris species column is not used by the algorithm.

5.3   Initializing the K-Means Algorithm

In the last few sections we saw how the assign and update steps were performed. Both of these operate on clusters that already have observations assigned to them. We must therefore start in a state where observations are assigned to clusters.

In this section we will look at two different means of initializing the clusters randomly. The initialization step of K-Means is stochastic, or random. The update and assign steps are both deterministic. However, because the algorithm has a non-deterministic beginning, the entire algorithm is non-deterministic.

There are two very popular means of initializing the K-Means algorithm: the Random algorithm and the Forgy algorithm. The name of first method–"Random"–is a bit misleading, however, as both algorithms use random numbers.

5.3.1   Random K-Means Initialization

The random algorithm is very simple. You simply create the requested **K** number of clusters and assign random observations to each of these clusters. It is also important that we do not let any cluster have zero observations. Of course, **K** should never be higher than the number of observations. That is, you cannot cluster 30 observations into 50 clusters. It is also very important that the "random" initialization proceed directly to the update step. This allows the centroids to be calculated for the newly created clusters.

First, we calculate the number of dimensions the observations have. The K-Means algorithm requires that each dimension contain the same number of dimensions. This is simply the array length.

```
dimensions = theObservations.length;
```

Next, we must create **K** clusters. We loop from zero up to, but not including **K**.

```
for i from 0 to K
{
  clusters.add(new Cluster(dimensions));
}
```

We must now assign each of the observations to a random cluster. First, loop over all observations provided.

```
foreach (observation in theObservations)
{
```

Then, pick a random cluster. Assign a random integer between 0 and **K-1**. Add that observation to the cluster.

```
clusterIndex = randInt (K);
cluster = clusters [clusterIndex];
cluster.add(observation);
}
```

We can now handle any clusters that might have no observations assigned to them.

```
foreach (cluster in this.clusters)
{
 if (cluster.length == 0)
 {
```

It is time to add one observation to this cluster. We do not want to create another zero length cluster in the process of fixing this cluster, however. Find a random cluster that has more than one observation already. Make sure that the chosen cluster is not the same cluster as that we are trying to fill.

```
done = false;
while (!done)
{
   sourceIndex = randInt (K);
   source = clusters [sourceIndex];
   if (source != cluster && source.length > 1)
   {
```

Once we find the cluster, we can move the observation. Choose a random observation from the source cluster and move it to the empty cluster. We can now set the **done** flag to **true**.

```
   sourceObservationIndex = rndInt (source.length);
   sourceObservation = source [sourceObservationIndex];
   source.remove(sourceObservationIndex);
   cluster.add(sourceObservation);
   done = true;
  }
 }
 }
}
updateStep ();
```

Once the observations have been assigned to their clusters, we can perform the update step.

Figure 5.2 shows the flow chart for a K-Means algorithm that uses random initialization.

Figure 5.2: Random Initialization

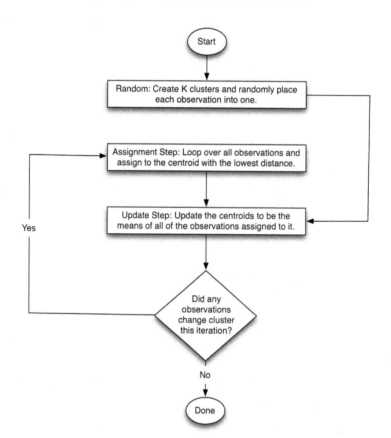

Note that the random initialization goes directly to update form initialization. Performing the assignment step after a random initialization would not make sense, because the initialization step already assigned the observations to clusters. You will see in the next section that the for Forgy K-Means initialization has a slightly different flow.

5.3.2 Forgy K-Means Initialization

Forgy initialization works by first establishing the centroid values and then assigning the observations to the nearest clusters. This is done using the pseudo code described below. First, determine the number of dimensions in the observations. Each observation should have the same number of dimensions. We will also keep a hash set of **usedObservations**. We will not use every observation for initialization, but we do not want to reuse an observation, either.

```
dimensions = theObservations.length;
usedObservations = new HashSet();
```

We now loop through and create **K** clusters.

```
for i from 0 to K
```

Create the cluster, with the correct number of dimensions.

```
cluster = new Cluster(dimensions);
clusters.add(cluster);
```

With the cluster created, select a random observation. Do not choose an observation that has already been used.

```
observationIndex = -1;

while (observationIndex == -1)
{
  observationIndex = randInt(theObservations.length);
  if (usedObservations.contains(observationIndex))
  {
    observationIndex = -1;
  }
}
```

Now we have a random observation that was not previously used. Create a cluster with only that observation and assign that observation to the cluster's centroid.

```
observation = theObservations[observationIndex];
usedObservations.add(observationIndex);
}
```

Figure 5.3 shows the flow of an application that uses Forgy initialization.

Figure 5.3: Forgy Initialization

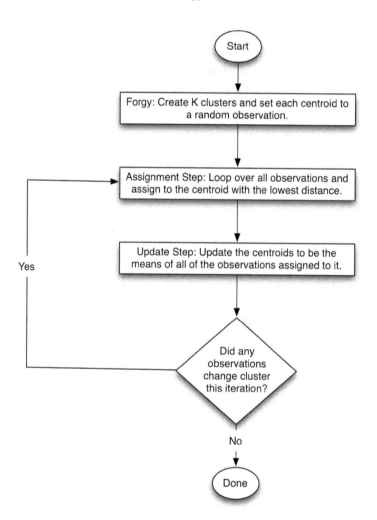

As you can see from the above figure, the assignment step is processed right after the initialization step. This is because Forgy has already set up the cluster centroids, and we now need to assign all of the observations to the clusters.

5.4   Chapter Summary

Clustering is a method for placing observations into clusters. The similarity between observations determines what observations are placed into what clusters. Clustering is an example of unsupervised training.

There are a number of different algorithms for clustering. One of the most popular is the K-Means algorithm. The K-Means algorithm assigns the observations into a fixed number of clusters. It takes several iterations for K-Means to move all of the observations into acceptable clusters. You should iterate the K-Means algorithm until you have an iteration where no observation changes clusters.

There are three different steps that are used in the K-Means algorithm. The initialization step creates the initial clusters. The assignment step updates the centroid for each cluster. The centroid is the vector average of all observations assigned to that cluster. The update step recalculates all centroid values based on observations assigned to those clusters.

This chapter introduced you to clustering and unsupervised training. In the next chapter, you will learn about error calculation. Error calculation is primarily used in supervised training. It helps to calculate the difference between the actual output and the ideal output of a machine learning method.

Chapter 6

Error Calculation

- Supervised Training

- Sum of Squares Error (SSE)

- Mean Squares (MSE)

- Root Mean Squares

- Data Sets

Error calculation is very important for supervised training. A training set for supervised training consists of vector pairs. These pairs align input vectors with an output, or ideal, vector that is the expected response to the provided input vectors.

Listing 6.1 shows an example of how vector pairs would be constructed for the XOR function.

Listing 6.1: The XOR Function/Operator

```
Input:  [0,0];  Ideal:  [0]
Input:  [0,1];  Ideal:  [1]
Input:  [1,0];  Ideal:  [1]
Input:  [1,1];  Ideal:  [0]
```

The XOR function always returns **true** when the two inputs are different. If the two inputs are the same, then it returns **false**. In the above listing, **true** is normalized to 1 and **false** to 0. The above training set would be used to teach a machine-learning algorithm to emulate the XOR function. This is a common introductory task for machine learning algorithms.

In the above listing, there are two inputs: 0 and 1. The ideal output for each of the four input vectors is also provided. This training set contains four input/ideal output pairs.

There are a variety of different error calculation methods that are commonly used with machine learning algorithms. In this chapter we will look at the following three error calculation methods:

- Sum of Squares Error (SSE)

- Mean Square Error (MSE)

- Root Mean Square Error (RMS)

The most commonly used error calculation method is Mean Square Error (MSE). However, this does not mean the MSE should always be used. Sometimes, the machine-learning algorithm in use will dictate the error calculation method that you should use. You can also use multiple error calculation methods if necessary, for comparison.

The following sections will describe each of these error calculation methods.

6.1   Sum of Squares Error

The Sum of Squares Error (SSE) is a very simple error calculation method used by some machine learning algorithms. A high SSE value indicates that there is a large difference between the expected output and the actual output. A training algorithm should work to minimize SSE.

The calculation of SSE is shown in Equation 6.1. (Draper, 1998)

$$\text{SSE} = \sum_i \left(\hat{y}_i - \bar{y}_i \right)^2 \tag{6.1}$$

Where **y hat** is the ideal output and **y bar** is the actual output.

The most common reason to use SSE is that some training algorithms require it. SSE is essentially the sum of squares of the individual variances of each output. Because of this, bigger training sets will always tend to have larger SSE values. This is one of the weaknesses of the SSE value–you cannot directly compare the SSE values from two training sets of different sizes.

6.2 Root Mean Square

The Root Mean Square (RMS) error calculation method is similar to the SSE method in that it is based on the squares of the individual differences between expected output vectors and the actual output. However, a mean is taken of all of these squares and then the square root is taken of this mean. Because the RMS is based on a mean, you can compare the RMS values of two different training sets. (Draper, 1998)

$$\text{RMS} = \sqrt{\frac{1}{n} \sum_{i=1}^{n} \left(\hat{y}_i - \bar{y} \right)^2} \tag{6.2}$$

Where **y hat** is the ideal output and **y bar** is the actual output.

6.3 Mean Square Error

MSE error calculation is the most commonly used error calculation for machine learning. Most, but not all, Internet examples of neural networks, support vector machines, and other models make use of MSE. MSE is shown in Equation 6.3. (Draper, 1998)

$$\text{MSE} = \frac{1}{n} \sum_{i=1}^{n} \left(\hat{y}_i - \bar{y}_i \right)^2 \tag{6.3}$$

Where **y hat** is the ideal output and **y bar** is the actual output.

The mean square error is essentially the mean of the squares of the individual differences. Because the individual differences are squared, it does not matter to MSE if the difference is positive or negative.

You may be wondering how to choose between RMS and MSE. RMS and MSE are very similar. One important difference is that RMS is linear whereas MSE is not. If you were to double every error in the training set, the RMS errors would also double, while the MSE errors would not. Sometimes it is useful to be able to compare errors like this.

6.4   Comparison of Error Calculation Methods

This section shows how to add random distortion to a training set. Listing 6.2 shows how small, medium, large, and huge distortions affect each of the training sets.

Listing 6.2: Error Calculation Methods

Type	SSE	MSE	RMS
Small	2505	0.01	0.1
Medium	62634	0.251	0.501
Large	250538	1.002	1.001
Huge	25053881	100.216	10.011

The largest effect is on the SSE error calculation, because SSE is a simple summation of the errors. SSE has a larger change than RMS. You can see that RMS is essentially the square root of MSE.

6.4.1   Partitioning Training Data

You typically do not want to use all available data for training, as there is almost always noise in your data. The word "noise" is used to describe small distortions that are not consistently reproducible. A successfully trained algorithm will be able to see through the noise and still predict accurately. Over fitting occurs when the algorithm memorizes the noise. Because the noise is not consistent, this will greatly impair the algorithm's ability to recognize data outside of the training set. Because noise is not consistent, it will cause the algorithm to see false patterns. Such patterns create a phenomenon called training set bias.

Selection bias is another concern. If you need to choose from among several competing machine learning algorithms, you should not simply choose the algorithm that trained to the lowest error, or you will likely pick the most over fit model.

Available data is typically broken into three sets to avoid bias. It is important that these sets are randomly sampled from available data, as you do not want to introduce any bias when selecting the items for each set. Randomly select items from the available data in order to avoid bias. For time-series data, you select chronological ranges. The three sets that training data is typically divided into are listed here.

- Training set

- Validation set

- Test set

The training set is the data with which you train your algorithm. This is usually the largest of three sets. Training data is often selected as 80% of available data. You can then split the remaining 20% between validation and test. It is important to remember that error on your training data is often very optimistic. This is because the training data was used to train the algorithm.

If you are evaluating several different algorithms, you should use the test set next to see what algorithms learned the best. Use data that the algorithms did not see during the training, as the algorithms should be unbiased to this data.

6.5   Chapter Summary

This chapter introduced supervised training, using data sets. A supervised data set is used with a supervised training algorithm and contains pairs of vectors. Each of these pairs represents one element in the training set. Each pair contains an input vector and an output vector that represents the expected output from that input vector. Machine learning algorithms are evaluated based on how closely the actual output matches the ideal expected output.

There are several different error calculation algorithms. One of the most basic is the Sum of Squares Error (SSE). This method calculates the difference between the actual and expected outputs for the machine-learning algorithm. The SSE algorithm then squares and sums each of these differences.

The Mean Squares Error (MSE) is one of the most commonly used distance calculation methods in machine learning. This calculation is similar to SSE; however, MSE is divided by the number of elements, thus producing an average.

Once you have selected your algorithm, you can use the test set to give you an idea of how well the algorithm might perform with real data. This should be the final indicator of the overall performance of your chosen model. MSE is not linear–if the difference doubles, MSE will not double.

The Root Mean Square (RMS) error is essentially the square root of the MSE error. Unlike MSE, RMS is linear. This allows you to directly evaluate two RMS errors. If the difference between the actual and ideal vectors doubles, then RMS will also double.

This chapter introduced several concepts in supervised training and described how to construct supervised training sets. It also discussed several methods for evaluating these data sets. The next chapter introduces machine learning. You will see how simple models can be constructed and trained to produce the correct output.

Chapter 7

Towards Machine Learning

- Training a Polynomial

- Greedy Random Training

- RBF Functions

- RBF Network Model

In previous chapters we saw that a machine-learning algorithm typically accepts an input vector and produces an output vector. To transform this input vector into an output vector, two additional vectors can be used. These additional vectors are referred to as long-term and short-term memory. Long-term memory can also be referred to as weights or coefficients. It is adjusted through training. Short-term memory is not used by all machine-learning algorithms.

It might be helpful to think of a machine-learning algorithm as a function. We will treat a very simple equation as though it were a machine-learning algorithm in equation 7.1, in order to demonstrate.

$$f(x) = 5x \tag{7.1}$$

Here we think of $\mathbf{x}$ as a single value–a scalar, rather than a vector. The value 5 is a coefficient. Coefficients are usually grouped into a vector and represent the long-term memory of the algorithm. When we train Equation

7.1, we will adjust the coefficient until we arrive at a value that produces the desired output. If Listing 7.1 represented the training data for the algorithm of Equation 7.1, we could feed the input into Equation 7.1 and evaluate the results.

Listing 7.1: Simple Training Data

```
Input:  [1], Desired Output:  [7]
Input:  [2], Desired Output:  [14]
Input:  [3], Desired Output:  [21]
```

The coefficient of 5 would not provide the desired output. As we saw in Chapter 6, we could calculate the error between the above desired outputs and the actual outputs provided in Listing 7.1. For example, the input of 1 to Equation 7.1 would produce 5, while our desired output for 1 is 7.

There are many different ways to find a suitable coefficient for machine learning algorithms. Coefficient adjustment methods is one of the primary areas of research for machine learning.

If the machine learning algorithm is a linear function, as is the case with Equation 7.1, mathematical techniques can often be used to find a suitable coefficient. For this simple case, we only need to find the coefficient that yields 7 when multiplied by 1. This coefficient would be 7. A coefficient of 7 also yields a zero error for the other training set elements.

Not all data sets will be so easy. In fact, it is extremely rare to fit the coefficients (or long-term memory vectors) to result in an error that is exactly zero. This is because most data contains noise. Noise is any outcome that is not consistently reproducible given its input data, and thus contributes to a higher error rate. The goal of a machine learning algorithm is usually for the algorithm to perform well on new data, rather than displaying zero error.

If you do get a zero error, you should be suspicious that your coefficients are over fit. Over fitting occurs when the machine learning method has memorized your training data. At this point, the algorithm simply recalls memorized input vectors rather than learning to abstract output. An over fit algorithm will not perform well on new data that is not in the original training set.

We will now look at some methods for optimizing the coefficients to lower the error and be introduced to a few foundational algorithms for optimizing the coefficients. The next chapters will discuss more advanced algorithms, such as simulated annealing and Nelder Mead.

Most training algorithms presented in this book are generic. Given any long-term memory vector, these algorithms can attempt to optimize. This is not the case with every training algorithm, however. Some training algorithms use specific insights into the algorithm that they are trying to train. We will see such algorithms in Chapter 10. However, most of the algorithms in the other chapters of this book are generic.

7.1   Coefficients of a Polynomial

This section describes how to implement a generic training method in order to optimize the coefficients of a polynomial. We will use the polynomial as the machine-learning algorithm that we seek to optimize. Typically, you will optimize the coefficients into something more complex than a simple polynomial, but this example will serve as a great introduction to machine learning. Fitting a polynomial to a dataset illustrates the fundamentals of how more complex machine learning algorithms work.

A polynomial is a mathematical expression consisting of variables and constant coefficients and uses only the operations of addition, subtraction, multiplication, and positive integer exponents. Equation 7.2 shows a typical, second degree polynomial. (Lial, 2010)

$$f(x) = 2x^2 + 4x + 6 \tag{7.2}$$

The above mathematical function accepts a value **x** and returns a value **y**. The input and output vectors for this function are both of size one. There are three coefficients in Equation 7.1: 2, 4, and 6. In this case, the coefficients are multiplied against the variable **x**. The coefficient 2 is multiplied against **x** squared, the coefficient 4 is multiplied against **x**. Even 6 is a coefficient. Technically 6 is multiplied against **x** to the power of zero. Though **x** to the power of zero is equal to one.

The above polynomial is said to be of the "second degree" because there are three terms. Each term relates to a coefficient. The three coefficients used in Equation 7.1 can be thought of as a vector and described as follows:

```
[2 ,4 ,6]
```

For Equation 7.1, the coefficient is already specified. Often we will need to use machine learning to determine what the coefficient(s) should be. To do so, you would use a training set that includes the expected outputs for a variety of inputs. Such data can be collected experimentally. In order to fit these observations to a second degree polynomial, we can use machine learning to help.

We will begin by creating some training data. We already know that we want the solution to be the coefficients [2,4,6]. This is a completely contrived example, but it will demonstrate how to use some basic training algorithms. To generate the training data, loop over some **x** values and calculate the polynomial for each. Then, use random coefficients to train to the correct coefficients. We will use only the training data to see if we can rebuild the correct coefficients.

The generated training data is shown in Listing 7.2. As you can see, we loop the input from -50 to +50 and calculate the ideal output.

Listing 7.2: Polynomial Training Data

```
[BasicData: input:[−50.0], ideal:[4806.0]]
[BasicData: input:[−49.0], ideal:[4612.0]]
[BasicData: input:[−48.0], ideal:[4422.0]]
...
[BasicData: input:[47.0], ideal:[4612.0]]
[BasicData: input:[48.0], ideal:[4806.0]]
[BasicData: input:[49.0], ideal:[5004.0]]
```

Given the above data, we will now see how the coefficients can be adjusted to produce the above data. In the next section we will see how we can use the training data in Listing 7.2 to reconstruct the polynomial. Of course, we will assume that we did not know the actual polynomial in the first place. We only assume we have Listing 7.2.

7.2   Introduction to Training

There are many different ways to adjust the long-term memory of a machine-learning algorithm during training. In this section, we will look at greedy random training. This method is simple to implement. In the next chapter, we will look at more robust training algorithms. Robust training algorithms will typically find an optimal setting for long-term memory faster than greedy random training.

7.2.1   Greedy Random Training

Greedy random training is extremely simple to implement. Essentially, all it does is randomly select values for the long-term memory vector. This algorithm is greedy in the sense that it only accepts a new memory vector if the new vector is an improvement over the previous one. This algorithm keeps choosing new random values for the long-term memory and always maintains the best vector seen so far. This algorithm is sometimes called a random walk.

This algorithm can be seen in the pseudo code shown in Listing 7.3.

Listing 7.3: Greedy Random Training (minimize score)

```
function iteration(
 ltm, // the current long term memory vector
 lowRange, // the lowest value to randomize to
 highRange // the highest value to randomize to
)
{
 // Score the current state.
 oldScore = calculateScore(ltm);
 // Keep a copy of the current state, in case we
 // fail to improve it.
 len = ltm.length;
 oldLtm = ltm.clone();

 // Set to a random state.
 for i from 0 to len
 {
 ltm[i] = rand(lowRange, highRange);
 }
 // Score the new random vector.
 newScore = calculateScore(ltm);
 // Greedy decision. Did the randomization improve our state?
 // If not, then back it out.
 if( newScore > oldScore )
 {
 Ltm = oldLtm.clone();
 }
}
```

The above code implements one iteration of a greedy random algorithm. There are three parameters that you pass to the above function.

- Parameter 1. The long-term memory vector that you would like to optimize.

- Parameters 2 & 3. The low and high ranges for the values that you would like to randomly assign to the individual elements in the long-term memory vector.

The iteration function then assigns random values to the long-term memory vector. The score of the vector is compared to the score from before the randomization. If the vector's score did not decrease, then throw out the changes and revert to the previous vector. This is why it is called greedy. It will only accept improvements. This is not always the best policy. As the old saying goes, "sometimes you have to take one step backward to take two steps forward."

Believe it or not, the greedy random trainer can actually train vectors. Running it against the polynomial (from Equation 7.2) yields the following results.

```
Iteration #999984, Score=37.93061791363337,
Iteration #999985, Score=37.93061791363337,
Iteration #999986, Score=37.93061791363337,
Iteration #999987, Score=37.93061791363337,
Iteration #999988, Score=37.93061791363337,
Iteration #999989, Score=37.93061791363337,
Iteration #999990, Score=37.93061791363337,
Iteration #999991, Score=37.93061791363337,
Iteration #999992, Score=37.93061791363337,
Iteration #999993, Score=37.93061791363337,
Iteration #999994, Score=37.93061791363337,
Iteration #999995, Score=37.93061791363337,
Iteration #999996, Score=37.93061791363337,
Iteration #999997, Score=37.93061791363337,
Iteration #999998, Score=37.93061791363337,
Iteration #999999, Score=37.93061791363337,
Iteration #1000000, Score=37.93061791363337,
Final score: 37.93061791363337
2.0026889363153195x^2+4.057350732096355x+9.393343096548456
```

As you can see, the greedy random training algorithm came reasonably close to the expected coefficients. Instead of getting [2,4,6], we got [2.002, 4.057, and 9.3933].

The greedy random algorithm is often used as a benchmark. You can compare the greedy random result against a new algorithm that you are evaluating. If the new algorithm does not outperform the greedy random algorithm, then you know the new algorithm is performing very poorly.

7.3 Radial Basis Networks

In the last section we looked at how to optimize the coefficients for a polynomial. Most machine learning algorithms are much more complex than a simple polynomial. In this section we will introduce an RBF Network. (Bishop, 1996) The RBF network is a statistical model that can be used both for regression and classification.

There are many different methods for training an RBF network. The RBF network has a vector that represents its long-term memory. For an RBF network, the long-term memory is a combination of coefficients and other parameters. There is no short-term memory vector for the RBF network. It can be trained by both greedy random and hill climbing algorithms, and is based on radial basis functions (RBF).

The next section will briefly review RBFs and describe the exact makeup of this vector.

7.3.1 Radial Basis Functions

Radial basis functions are a very important concept in AI, as many different AI algorithms make use of them. There are a number of different RBF types, several of which will be introduced in this chapter.

A radial basis function is symmetric about its center, which is typically located somewhere along the x-axis. The RBF will reach its maximum value at the center. This maximum value is called the peak, and is often set to one. In the context of RBF networks, the peak is always set to one and the center varies accordingly.

RBFs can have many dimensions. The output of an RBF will always be a single scalar value, regardless of the number of dimensions in the vector passed to the RBF.

There are a number of commonly used RBFs. We will start with the most common: the Gaussian function. Figure 7.1 shows a graph of a 1D Gaussian function centered at 0.

Figure 7.1: Gaussian Function

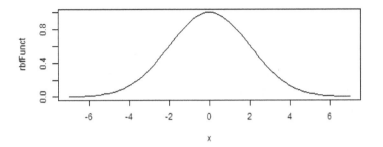

RBF functions are commonly used to selectively scale something, and Gaussian is no different. Consider Figure 7.1. If this function were used to scale something, you would have maximum intensity at the center. The intensity would fall off in either the positive or negative directions as you moved from the center.

Before we can look at the equation for the Gaussian RBF, we must consider how to process the multiple dimensions. It is important to note that RBFs accept multi-dimensional input to return a single value. It does this by calculating the distance between the input and the center vector of the RBF. This distance is called **r**. The RBF center and input to the RBF must always have the same number of dimensions for the calculation to occur. Once we calculate **r**, then we can calculate the individual RBF function. All of the RBF functions make use of this calculated **r**.

Equation 7.3 shows how to calculate **r**.

$$r = ||\mathbf{x} - \mathbf{x}_i||\tag{7.3}$$

The double vertical bars you see in the equation above represent that the function describes a distance. Euclidean distance is almost always used for an RBF. However, other distances might be used for certain very specialized cases. The examples provided for this book always use the Euclidean distance. Therefore, **r** is simply the Euclidean distance between the center and the **x** vector. The value **r** will be used in each of the RBF functions used in this section.

The equation for a Gaussian RBF is shown in Equation 7.4.

$$\phi(r) = e^{-r^2}\tag{7.4}$$

Once you've calculated r, it is fairly easy to calculate the RBF. The Greek letter PHI, which you see at the left of the equation, always represents an RBF.

The Gaussian is not the only RBF, and other RBFs have different shapes. If you are using the RBF to scale, these different shapes can give you different ways to scale a number. Figure 7.2 shows the Ricker Wavelet.

Figure 7.2: The Ricker Wavelet (Mexican Hat Function)

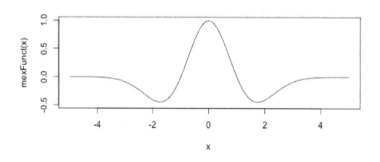

The Ricker Wavelet is often used as an RBF. It is often called the Mexican hat function, due to its pictorial resemblance to a sombrero. The equation for the Ricker Wavelet is provided in Equation 7.5.

$$\phi(r) = (1 - r^2) \cdot e^{-r^2/2} \tag{7.5}$$

As you can see from Figure 7.2, the Ricker Wavelet actually scales negatively just at the edges, and then returns to zero.

Different RBF functions are useful in different situations. Some other common RBF functions include:

- Multiquadric

- Inverse quadratic

- Inverse multiquadric

- Polyharmonic spline

- Thin plate spline

We can make use of the RBF function to implement a statistical model called the RBF network. We will be able to train this model using any of the techniques discussed so far.

7.3.2   Radial Basis Function Networks

A Radial Basis Function network is a statistical model that can be used for both classification and regression. It provides a weighted summation of one or more Radial Basis Functions, each of which receives the weighted input attributes used to predict the output. The following equation describes an RBF network.

$$f(X) = \sum_{i=1}^{N} a_i p(||b_i X - c_i||) \qquad (7.6)$$

Note that the double vertical bars above mean to take the distance. Such symbols do not specify what distance algorithm to use; this is your choice. In the above equation $\mathbf{X}$ is the input vector of attributes, $\mathbf{c}$ is the vector center of the RBF, $\mathbf{p}$ is the chosen RBF (Gaussian, for example), $\mathbf{a}$ is the vector coefficient (or weight) for each RBF, and $\mathbf{b}$ specifies the vector coefficient to weight the input attributes. We will see pseudo code for Equation 7.6 later in this chapter.

In our example, we will apply the RBF network to the iris data set. Figure 7.3 provides a graphic representation of this application.

Figure 7.3: An RBF Network for the Iris Data

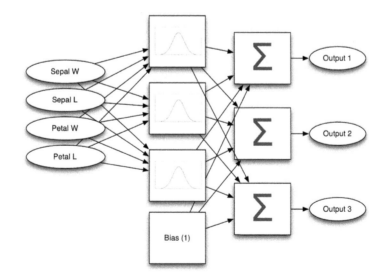

The above network contains four inputs (the length and width of petals and sepals), which map to the features that describe each iris species. The above diagram assumes that we are using one-of-n encoding for the three different iris species. It would also be possible to use equilateral encoding and have only two outputs. To keep things simple, however, we will use one-of-n. We also choose to use three RBF functions. This is purely an arbitrary choice. Additional RBF functions allow the model to learn more complex data sets. However, more RBF's take more time to process.

Arrows represent all coefficients from the equation. The arrows between the input attributes and RBFs are represented by **b** in Equation 7.6. Similarly, the arrows between the RBFs and the summation are represented by **a**. You will also note that there is a bias box. This is a synthetic function that always returns a value of 1. Because the bias function's output is constant, no inputs are required. The weights from the bias to the summation function very similarly to the vector intercept in linear regression. Bias is not always bad! In this case it is an important component to the RBF network. Bias nodes are also very common in neural networks.

Because there are multiple summations, you can see that this poses a classification problem. The highest summation specifies the predicted class. If this were a regression problem, there would be single output. The single output would represent the predicted output for regression.

You will also notice that there is a bias node in Figure 7.3. The bias node is located in the place where an additional RBF function might go. However, the bias node does not accept any input–unlike an RBF. The bias node always outputs a constant value of one. Of course, this constant value of 1 is multiplied by a coefficient value. This has the effect of the coefficient always being directly added to the output, regardless of the input. Bias nodes are very useful when the input is zero, as they allow the RBF layer to output values even when the input is zero.

The long-term memory vector for the RBF network is made up of several different components:

- Input coefficients

- Output/Summation coefficients

- RBF width scalars (same width in all dimensions)

- RBF center vectors

The RBF network will store all of these components as a single vector. This vector becomes the long-term memory of the RBF network. We will then make use of either greedy random or hill climbing training to set the vector to values that will produce the correct iris species for the features presented.

This model works almost exactly like the polynomial that we saw before. The only difference is that the equation is much more complex, as we now must calculate several output values and RBF functions.

7.3.3 Implementing an RBF Network

This section outlines the pseudo code for two major functions in the implementation of an RBF network. First, we will look at the function that initializes an RBF network. This function allocates the long-term memory vector that is used for the RBF network. To create the RBF network, you must provide the following three pieces of information.

- Input count

- RBF count

- Output count

The input and output counts simply specify the sizes of the input and output vectors. Your data set will dictate these values. The RBF count is a bit more subjective. The more RBF functions you have, the better the model will be able to predict desired outcomes. However, using more RBF functions increases inefficiency.

Listing 7.4 shows how an RBF network is initialized.

Listing 7.4: Initializing an RBF Network

```
function initRBFNetwork(
 theInputCount, // the number of inputs to the network
 rbfCount, // the number of RBF functions in the network
 theOutputCount // the output count
 )
{
 result = new RBFNetwork();
 // set simple properties on the network
 result.inputCount = theInputCount;
 result.outputCount = theOutputCount;
 // Calculate input and output weight counts.
 // Add 1 to output to account for an extra bias node.
 inputWeightCount = inputCount * rbfCount;
 outputWeightCount = (rbfCount + 1) * outputCount;
 rbfParams = (inputCount + 1) * rbfCount;

 // allocate enough space for the long term memory
 result.longTermMemory = alloc(inputWeightCount
 + outputWeightCount + rbfParams);
 // Set more properties on the model
 result.indexInputWeights = 0;
 result.indexOutputWeights = inputWeightCount + rbfParams;
 // Allocate RBF functions
 result.rbf = new FnRBF[rbfCount];
 // Set up all of the RBF functions
 for i from 0 to rbfCount
 {
   // The index for the current RBF function.
   rbfIndex = inputWeightCount + ((inputCount + 1) * i);
   // allocate a Gaussian and specify the input count and
   // the location in long term memory where this RBF
   // function's parameters are stored. The parameters are
   // the width, followed by the center dimensions.
   result.rbf[i] = new GaussianFunction(
     inputCount, result.longTermMemory, rbfIndex);
 }
 // return the newly constructed network
 return result;
}
```

The method begins by allocating an object named **result** to hold the RBF Network. This object will hold the long-term memory and a few other basic items about the network.

The above code calculates exactly how much long-term memory is needed to hold the coefficients and RBF parameters. The individual RBF functions are then allocated and pointed to the long-term memory for their parameters. The RBF parameters are their widths, followed by their center dimensions.

The above code does not actually fill the long-term memory with any values. Once the network has been allocated, you will typically assign it to random values. This will give the RBF network an initial starting point. Training will refine the long-term memory values into useful values that produce output closer to the expected outputs. For the iris data, these are the outputs that define what species the network thinks the inputs correspond to.

Once the RBF network has been set up and the long-term memory has been set, the network is ready for training. We will call the RBF model and score how well the initial outputs match up. Of course, we are starting with random values, so the output will not be good. However, you have to start somewhere.

Just as was done for the polynomial, we must calculate the output for the RBF network. The pseudo code in Listing 7.5 is provided to show the calculation in this context.

Listing 7.5: Calculating an RBF Network

```
function computeRBFNetwork(
 input, // the input vector
 network // the RBF network
 )
{
 // First, compute the output values of each of the RBFs.
 // Add one additional RBF output for bias (always set
 // to one).
 rbfOutput = alloc(network.rbf.length + 1);
 // Bias is always valued 1.
 rbfOutput[rbfOutput.length - 1] = 1;
 for rbfIndex from 0 to network.rbf.length
 {
   // weight the input
   weightedInput = alloc(input.length);
   for inputIndex from 0 to input.length
   {
     memoryIndex = network.indexInputWeights
     + (rbfIndex * network.inputCount) + inputIndex;
     weightedInput[inputIndex] = input[inputIndex]
       * network.longTermMemory[memoryIndex];
   }
   // calculate the rbf
   rbfOutput[rbfIndex] =
   network.rbf[rbfIndex].evaluate(weightedInput);
 }
 // Calculate the output, which is the result
 // of the weighted result of the RBFs.
 result = alloc(network.outputCount);
 for outputIndex from 0 to result.length
 {
   sum = 0;
   for rbfIndex from 0 to rbfOutput.length
   {
     // Add 1 to rbf length for bias.
     memoryIndex = network.indexOutputWeights
       + (outputIndex * (network.rbf.length + 1)) + rbfIndex;
     sum += rbfOutput[rbfIndex]
```

```
            * network.longTermMemory[memoryIndex];
        }
        result[outputIndex] = sum;
    }
    // finally, return the result.
    return result;
}
```

The above code calculates the final output in several layers. We create a variable named **rbfOutput**. As its name implies, it will hold the outputs from the RBF functions. We loop over all of the RBF functions and calculate the weighted input to the RBF. The weighted input is simply a vector created by multiplying each input by that RBF function's input coefficients. On Figure 7.3, these are the coefficients represented by the vertical group of arrows closest to the left. As each RBF function is calculated, the **rbfOutput** vector is filled, except for the last element of the **rbfOutput** vector. The last element gets a 1 and functions as the bias node.

Once the **rbfOutput** vector has been filled, it is multiplied by the output coefficients. The output coefficients are represented by the vertical column of arrows closest to the right in Figure 7.3. The calculated output values are placed into the result vector, and then the result vector is returned to the calling function.

7.3.4   Using an RBF Network

Examples for using RBF networks with the iris data set, as well as the XOR
data set, are provided below. These allow you to see how the RBF network
can be trained to learn the expected output for both XOR and iris. First, we
will look at the output from the XOR training with greedy random training.

```
Iteration #999996, Score=0.013418057671024912,
Iteration #999997, Score=0.013418057671024912,
Iteration #999998, Score=0.013418057671024912,
Iteration #999999, Score=0.013418057671024912,
Iteration #1000000, Score=0.013418057671024912,
Final score: 0.013418057671024912
[0.0, 0.0] -> [-0.16770550224628078], Ideal: [0.0]
[1.0, 0.0] -> [0.9067663351025073], Ideal: [1.0]
[0.0, 1.0] -> [0.8703332321473845], Ideal: [1.0]
[1.0, 1.0] -> [0.0064115711694006094], Ideal: [0.0]
```

Of course, many individual iterations were skipped. It also took a sizeable
number of iterations just to get the score down to 0.01. You can see from the
above output that the actual output does not exactly match the ideal. For the
first input of [0,0], we can see that the output should have been [0]; however,
it was -0.16, which is fairly close. The two outputs that should have been [1.0]
are both near 1.0, at 0.906 and 0.87.

Training to the iris data set provides the following output:

```
Iteration #99971, Score=0.08747428121794937,
Iteration #99972, Score=0.08747428121794937,
Iteration #99973, Score=0.08747428121794937,
Iteration #99974, Score=0.08747428121794937,
Iteration #99975, Score=0.08747428121794937,
Iteration #99976, Score=0.08747428121794937,
Iteration #99977, Score=0.08747428121794937,
Iteration #99978, Score=0.08747428121794937,
Iteration #99979, Score=0.08747428121794937,
Iteration #99980, Score=0.08747428121794937,
Iteration #99981, Score=0.08747428121794937,
Iteration #99982, Score=0.08747428121794937,
Iteration #99983, Score=0.08747428121794937,
Iteration #99984, Score=0.08747428121794937,
Iteration #99985, Score=0.08747428121794937,
```

```
Iteration  #99986,  Score =0.08747428121794937,
Iteration  #99987,  Score =0.08747428121794937,
Iteration  #99988,  Score =0.08747428121794937,
Iteration  #99989,  Score =0.08747428121794937,
Iteration  #99990,  Score =0.08747428121794937,
Iteration  #99991,  Score =0.08747428121794937,
Iteration  #99992,  Score =0.08747428121794937,
Iteration  #99993,  Score =0.08747428121794937,
Iteration  #99994,  Score =0.08747428121794937,
Iteration  #99995,  Score =0.08747428121794937,
Iteration  #99996,  Score =0.08747428121794937,
Iteration  #99997,  Score =0.08747428121794937,
Iteration  #99998,  Score =0.08747428121794937,
Iteration  #99999,  Score =0.08747428121794937,
Iteration  #100000,  Score =0.08747428121794937,
Final  score:  0.08747428121794937
```

The above shows that the training continued until the score reached 0.08. This allowed the majority of the irises to be correctly classified, and was the result of using greedy random training and a very large number of iterations. In the next chapter, we will get even better results in fewer iterations using more advanced training algorithms.

7.4   Chapter Summary

This chapter introduced you to the fundamentals of training machine learning algorithms. Once trained, the machine learning algorithm should be able to produce output close to what you would expect from the input. When input is provided with the expected output, the algorithm has been provided with a training set. Training sets are used to train the algorithms.

Most machine learning algorithms keep a long-term memory, which is adjusted when the algorithm is trained. This long-term memory is often referred to as a weight or coefficient, and is typically stored in a vector.

This chapter described the greedy random training algorithm. The greedy random training algorithm is a very simple training algorithm that assigns random values to long-term memory. New configurations are tried repeatedly and the best configuration is kept. This is a very simple training algorithm that is often used as a baseline against which one might benchmark other algorithms.

We trained two different models in this chapter: a simple polynomial and an RBF model. The polynomial demonstrated how the greedy random algorithm can be applied to very simple equations. We were able to approximate the three coefficients used in the polynomial.

The RBF model is based on radial basis functions, which are symmetric about a center. The RBF each have multi-dimensional centers and adjustable width values, although the width of an RBF is consistent across all dimensions. In this chapter, we used a Gaussian RBF.

The RBF model can be used for classification or regression and uses training algorithms to modify its long-term memory. The long-term memory for the RBF model is made up coefficients, RBF widths, and RBF centers. The RBF model was used to learn the iris data set.

The next chapter will introduce additional optimization algorithms. These algorithms can be used to adjust the long-term memory vector used by the RBF network. They can be used on any algorithm that stores its state in a long-term memory-like vector. The next chapter will describe hill climbing, simulated annealing and Nelder Mead training algorithms.

Chapter 8

Optimization Training

- Hill Climbing

- Simulated Annealing

- Nelder Mead

This chapter will refine the concept of training a machine learning algorithm to provide more complex approaches than those described in the previous chapter. There are many different algorithms for training machine learning algorithms. The algorithms presented in this chapter do not require any specific insight into the long-term memory vector they are attempting to optimize. This makes them very versatile in terms of what they can train.

This chapter will focus on optimizing continuous vectors, which are those that are made up of floating point numbers. Chapter 9 will focus on discrete problems.

8.0.1 Hill Climbing Training

Hill climbing is only marginally more complex to implement than the greedy random algorithm. One of the main disadvantages of the greedy random algorithm is that there is no refinement. A random vector is chosen for the long term memory and then immediately replaced if a better random vector is found. It does not attempt to refine a potentially good solution, but looks for a better one at random.

Hill climbing works by refining the current vector, which is why the name is actually very descriptive of the algorithm. Imagine that you are randomly placed somewhere in the middle of hilly terrain and your goal is to climb to the highest location possible. You begin by looking at every location that you could reach in one step and then decide what step you are going to take. You always decide to take the step that moves you the highest. This process is repeated until you cannot find a higher step. Once you cannot find a higher step, the process terminates. With hill climbing, the process terminates at the nearest high point, which is often called a local maxima.

This process can also be run in reverse, if you seek to minimize. Instead of selecting the step that leads you to the highest possible position, you would select the step that leads you to the lowest position. The lowest position is called the local minima. Local minima and maxima are very important elements of training.

Using this same analogy, consider if you started out somewhere on the East Coast of the United States and used hill climbing to find the highest place. You would probably get stuck somewhere in the Appalachian mountains, as walking to higher ground when starting on the East Coast would lead you to these peaks, and once you reached the peaks there would be no way to step higher. However, they are not the highest ground in the world, or even in the United States.

This example presumes you are walking in a two dimensional space on the Earth's surface. The third dimension, or altitude, does not count because you cannot directly change your altitude. You cannot fly! Yet, altitude is the objective. Altitude changes based your movements in the x and y dimensions. Most machine learning applications will have much more than two dimensions. However, the principle is still the same–these applications just have more dimensions to search.

You will very likely never find a global maximum or minimum for anything but a very trivial algorithm. Rather, you should hope to find successively better local minima or maxima. If you find your training to be "stuck," you will sometimes have to randomize and start over. You were probably stuck in a local minima or maxima (that is, stuck in the Appalachians, instead of reaching the Himalayas). Hill climbing is greedy. Hill climbing would be unwilling to give up its spot on top of the Appalachians to ever find anything else.

The hill climbing algorithm is implemented in two separate functions. The first function performs an initialization for the hill climbing algorithm, while the second function shows an iteration. We begin with Listing 8.1, which shows one iteration of the hill climbing algorithm. (Russell, 2009)

Listing 8.1: Hill Climbing Algorithm (Initialization)

```
function initHillClimb(
 ltm, // the initial long term memory
 acceleration, // the acceleration
 initialVelocity // the initial step size in each dimension
)
{
 for i from 0 to ltm.length
 {
   stepSize[i] = initialVelocity;
 }
 candidate[0] = -acceleration;
 candidate[1] = -1 / acceleration;
 candidate[2] = 0;
 candidate[3] = 1 / acceleration;
 candidate[4] = acceleration;
}
```

There are several different implementations of the hill climbing algorithm; this implementation makes use of step size and acceleration. The algorithm assumes that it will accelerate when it is moving in a direction that is producing positive results.

Listing 8.1 sets up two vectors for the algorithm to use. The **stepSize** vector tracks how big a step the algorithm is able to move in each dimension. The parameter for this is defined by the term **initialVelocity**. The **candidate** vector defines five potential moves that the algorithm might take. The algorithm applies these candidate moves to each dimension. These potential moves are based on the **acceleration** parameter. The **acceleration** and **initialVelocity** parameters will affect the efficiency of your training. You will have to experiment with them in order to gain the best results.

Now that the algorithm has been initialized, we can begin processing iterations. Listing 8.2 shows the iteration function of the hill climbing algorithm.

Listing 8.2: Hill Climbing Algorithm Iteration

```
function iterateHillClimb(ltm)
{
 len = ltm.length;
// loop over all dimensions and try to improve each
 for i from 0 to len
 {
   best = -1;
// We are trying to minimize, so set the best score to +Infinit.
// Everything is lower than that! So we default to the first
// score considered.
 bestScore = +Infinity;
// Try each of the candidate moves for this dimension.
   for j from 0 to candidate.length
   {
// Try the move and score, but back out the move once scored.
     ltm[i] = ltm[i] + (stepSize[i] * candidate[j]);
     temp = score.calculateScore(ltm);
     ltm[i] = ltm[i] - (stepSize[i] * candidate[j]);
// Keep track of what dimension (if any) had the best
// improvement.
     if ( temp < bestScore)
     {
       bestScore = temp;
       best = j;
     }
   }

// Now that we are done with the current dimension, see if
// any other step produced a better result. If so, move
// in that direction.
   if (best != -1)
   {
     ltm[i] = ltm[i] + (stepSize[i] * candidate[best]);
     stepSize[i] = stepSize[i] * candidate[best];
   }
 }
}
```

The above iteration function should be called until calling it does not result in a move. Once no further movement is possible, the algorithm has reached the local minima. The above function is designed to minimize the score function. Adapting it to maximize is relatively simple. The examples provided for this example on GitHub support both minimization and maximization.

Hill climbing will typically perform better than the greedy random algorithm. However, like the greedy random algorithm, hill climbing is still typically used as a benchmark algorithm.

The hill climbing implementation shown here optimizes continuous data, which has an infinite number of values between any two values. A different algorithm is used for optimization of discrete values, which have a fixed count. For example, the number of cars in a parking lot is a discreet number–there are no fractional cars. Chapter 9 will describe how to optimize for discrete values.

8.1 Simulated Annealing

Scott Kirkpatrick and several other researchers developed simulated annealing in the mid-1970s. It was originally developed to better optimize the design of integrated circuit (IC) chips by simulating the process of annealing.

Annealing is the metallurgical process of heating up a solid and then cooling it slowly until it crystallizes. The atoms of such materials have high-energy values at very high temperatures. This gives the atoms a great deal of freedom in their ability to restructure themselves. As the temperature is reduced, the energy levels of the atoms decrease. If the cooling process is carried out too quickly–a situation called rapid quenching–many irregularities and defects will be seen in the crystal structure. Ideally, the temperature should be reduced slowly to allow a more consistent and stable crystal structure to form, which will increase the metal's durability.

Simulated annealing seeks to emulate the annealing process. It begins at a very high temperature, at which the long term memory values are allowed to assume a wide range of random values. As the training progresses, the "temperature" is allowed to fall, thus restricting the degree to which the memory are permitted to vary. This often leads the simulated annealing algorithm to a better solution, just as a metal achieves a better crystal structure through the annealing process. (Das, 2005)

8.1.1   Simulated Annealing Applications

Given a specified number of inputs for an arbitrary equation, simulated annealing can be used to determine what inputs will produce the minimum result for the equation. In the case of the traveling salesman, this equation is the calculation of the total distance the salesman must travel. It is the error calculation or scoring function for a machine-learning algorithm.

When simulated annealing was first introduced, the algorithm was very popular for integrated circuit (IC) chip design. Most IC chips are composed of many internal logic gates, which allow the chip to accomplish the tasks that it was designed to perform. Just as algebraic equations can often be simplified, so too can IC chip layouts.

Simulated annealing is often used to find an IC chip design that has fewer logic gates than the original. The result is a chip that generates less heat and runs faster. The long term memory vector of a machine learning algorithm provides an excellent vector to optimize. Different memory values are used for the algorithm until one is found that produces a sufficiently low return from the error function.

8.1.2   Simulated Annealing Algorithm

The simulated annealing algorithm is similar to hill climbing in that it considers what moves it can make from its current position. These moves are evaluated randomly. If the randomly chosen move has a better score, than the current position, then the algorithm moves to the new position. If the new position is a worse score, then the new position will be accepted with random probability. This random probability is higher if the temperature is higher, as summarized in Figure 8.1.

Figure 8.1: Simulated Annealing Flowchart

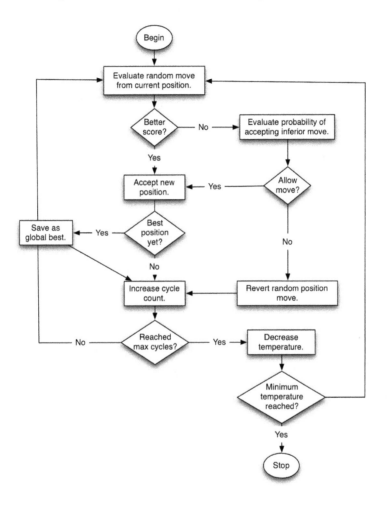

The ability to take on a worse score is an important distinction. Simulation annealing is not as greedy as the greedy random algorithm. Simulated annealing will sometimes take one step backwards to potentially take two steps forward.

The pseudo code to the complete algorithm is provided in Listing 8.3.

Listing 8.3: Simulated Annealing Pseudo Code

```
function iteration(
 ltm, // the long term memory we are trying to optimize
 cycles // the number of cycles per iteration
)
{
 len = ltm.length;
 k++;
 currentTemperature = coolingSchedule();
 for cycle from 0 to cycles
 {
// backup current state
 oldState = ltm.clone();
// randomize the method
    performRandomize(ltm);
// did we improve it? Only keep the new method
// if it improved (greedy).
      trialError = calculateScore(ltm);
// was this iteration an improvement? If so, always keep.
 keep = false;
 if trialError < currentError
 {
   keep = true;
 }
 else
 {
   p = calcProbability(
       currentError,
       trialError,
       currentTemperature);
   if (p > rand())
   {
     keep = true;
   }
 }
// should we keep this new position?
```

```
if (keep)
{
  currentError = trialError;
// better than global error
  if (trialError < globalBestError)
  {
    globalBestError = trialError;
    oldState = ltm.clone();
    globalBest = ltm.clone();
  }
}
else
{
  ltm = oldState.clone();
}
}
}
```

The above code performs one iteration of the simulated annealing algorithm. The iteration begins by obtaining the current temperature from the cooling schedule. This temperature will remain the same for the entire iteration. The iteration will execute a defined number of cycles. For each cycle, the algorithm will attempt to move from the current position. Each cycle will take place at the same temperature.

For each cycle, a random position is chosen. This random position is based on the current position. Because of this, only close positions will be considered. If the new position has a better score than the current position, then the algorithm moves to the new position. Otherwise, it calculates a probability based on the previous error, the current error, and the current temperature. The exact process used to calculate the probability will be described later in this chapter.

At the end of the iteration, the algorithm checks to see if it has surpassed any previous best solutions. In this regard, the algorithm is ultimately somewhat "greedy" in that it always keeps the best solution that it has found so far.

8.1.3   Cooling Schedule

The cooling schedule defines how quickly the temperature will fall during the simulated annealing iterations. The temperature determines the likelihood that an algorithm will move to a new position with a worse score. It is best if this probability is higher in the beginning phases of the training. Once the training has run for a longer time, it is best if the probability of moving to a worse position is much less. This allows the algorithm to narrow in on a more optimal solution. The following equation is used to calculate the cooling schedule.

$$T(k) = T_{init} \frac{T_{final}}{T_{init}}^{\frac{k}{k_{max}}} \tag{8.1}$$

The above equation calculates the temperature for iteration number **k**. There are a few things to keep in mind when setting the equation.

- The equation must also be provided with the initial and final temperatures, as well as the max number of iterations.

- It is not necessary that you use this equation exactly.

- It is important that the temperature decrease as training progresses.

- Do not choose zero as the final temperature in the above equation. It is okay to choose something close to zero, however. Because the above equation multiplies by the final temperature, having a final temperature of zero will quickly take the current temperature to zero.

You can see this cooling schedule in Figure 8.2.

Figure 8.2: Cooling from 1,000 to 10,500 Iterations

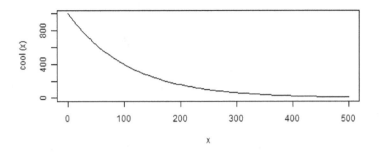

The temperature is used to determine the probability that the algorithm will accept an inferior score.

8.1.4 Annealing Probability

Simulated annealing always attempts to move the algorithm to random locations. Sometimes these random locations will not produce as good a score as the previous location. A completely greedy algorithm would never consider a new position that produces a worse score. However, such an outlook can be counterproductive. You might have to go through a few valleys before you find the top of the highest mountain!

We will compute the probability that the simulated annealing algorithm will accept a worse score as a function of the following three inputs:

- Current error

- Previous error

- Current temperature

Equation 8.2 makes use of all of these.

$$P(e, e', T) = \exp(-(e' - e)/T) \tag{8.2}$$

The probability function accepts the previous error, current error, and current temperature. The probability function returns a number between 0 and 1. A value of one means a 100% likelihood of selecting a worse score, and a value of zero means there is no likelihood of selecting a worse score. These numbers can easily be compared against random numbers. If the random number is less than the probability, then we will accept the solution with an inferior score.

Equation 8.2 returns higher probabilities for higher temperatures. However, the increase in error is also considered. The larger the increase in error, the new position is less likely to be accepted.

Simulated annealing can also be used to train the RBF networks introduced in the last chapter. It allows for more efficient learning than could be achieved with the hill climbing and greedy random algorithms alone.

8.2 Nelder Mead

The Nelder Mead algorithm was proposed by John Nelder and Roger Mead (Nelder, 1965). It is an optimization algorithm that can be used to optimize vectors to a scoring function. The Nelder Mead method is sometimes called the downhill simplex method or amoeba method. Nelder Mead is relatively easy to visualize and understand. It is also a generally effective solutions finder. It thus provides a great introduction to advanced training algorithms.

Nelder Mead works by constructing a simplex. A simplex is a geometric shape that has a number of vertices equal to N+1, where N is the number of dimensions in the problem. A vertex is a point in space. These vertices become the corners of a geometric shape called a simplex. Lines are drawn to form new shapes that connect vertices, or corners. If we were optimizing a vector with two dimensions, we would have a simplex in the shape of a triangle.

The simplex is simply a list of potential solutions. The algorithm always keeps N+1 potential solutions, and so the simplex will change its shape as training progresses. Once the training has reached an advanced state, the simplex has most become very small. At this point, we can find the solution by selecting the vertex with the best score.

The Nelder Mead algorithm can also be used to train the RBF networks introduced in the last chapter. It is able to converge to a low error faster than greedy random, hill climbing, and often simulated annealing algorithms.

Nelder Mead always begins with an initial guess as to the solution vector. If you cannot make an educated guess, then choose a random vector. If you previously trained with another algorithm, you can use your result from the last algorithm as the initial guess, and Nelder Mead will further refine the solution. This also works if you want to refine a previous Nelder Mead solution.

The initial solution becomes one of the vertices of the starting simplex. If we have two dimensions, then we need to generate two additional vertices. The simplex is always constructed of N+1 vertices, where N is the number of dimensions. It is important that you not confuse dimension with vertex. A vertex is a point made up of one or more dimensions.

We will now consider Nelder Mead for two dimensions. The following would be true in this case.

- Dimensions = N = 2

- Vertices = N+1 = 3 (a triangle)

- Simplex: A collection of 3 vertices, each having 2 dimensions (resulting in the shape of a triangle)

The first step for Nelder Mead is to generate the initial simplex. This simplex will be refined as the iterations progress. The initial simplex always takes the initial solution vector as one of the starting vertices. The other N vertices are created by moving one of the N dimensions by a set amount. Typically, the sides of the initial simplex are set to be of the same length.

Figure 8.3 shows a visualization of a three vertex simplex in two dimensions.

Figure 8.3: Nelder Mead Simplex

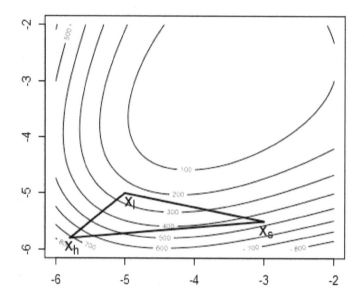

The above graph is a topology map. I sometimes like to think of the vertices in the above figure as members of a search party covering rugged terrain. All are looking for the optimal point on the map. The optimal point might be a high or a low, depending on how you define a good score. In a nutshell, Nelder Mead works by moving the searcher who is in the worst position to a new location that is based on the better positions of the other two.

The minimum that the depicted simplex is moving toward is in the large oval-like area in the top-right. The vertices are labeled **X**, although they are not to be confused with x and y dimensions. The three **X** vertices are labeled **h**, **s**, and **l**. They are the worst, second worst, and the best vertices, respectively.

Iterations of Nelder Mead consist of the following steps:

- Step 1. Find the worst, second worst, and best points of the vertex.

- Step 2. Reflect the worst to a better point through the best side.

- Step 3. If the reflection is successful, expand.

- Step 4. If the reflection it unsuccessful, contract.

8.2.1 Reflection

Reflection is the first step in the Nelder Mead algorithm. The worst vertex will be the one considering a move. Figure 8.4 shows the basic setup for moving by reflection.

Figure 8.4: Reflection

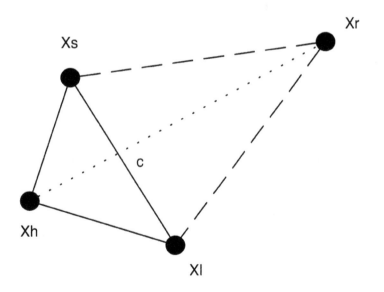

The current simplex is depicted by the solid lines, and the worst position is Xh. To reflect Xh, the average is taken between Xs and Xl. This gives a center, which is labeled as c in the figure above. If you consider the search party example, the farthest off searcher (Xh) looks in the direction of the other two and points at the center point (the average) between them as the best place to go. Because the other two are in better locations than him, the searcher must assume that anything behind him is also worse. He must move toward the other two, so he visualizes a point well beyond them, at point Xr. He visualizes a point well beyond because he aspires to become the best searcher!

After selecting the point at Xr, the point is now evaluated. Was it actually a better location? If it was, then we continue by implementing expansion. If not, then we continue by implementing contraction.

8.2.2   Expansion

Continuing the example from before, the Xh searcher has seen that he could improve his ranking by moving to Xr. Now he gets a little greedy, and wants to move farther. If we are climbing down a valley, then going to a farther point will probably get us to the optimal point faster. Figure 8.5 depicts this scenario.

Figure 8.5: Expansion

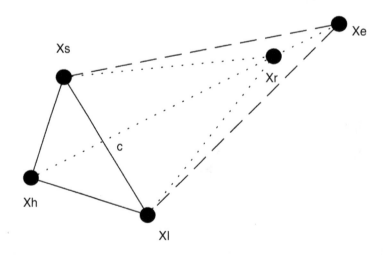

The searcher at Xh evaluated the spot at Xr. It was an improvement. So he became greedy and jumped right to Xe without checking Xe. This is okay, since even if he overshoots, he was at the worst spot to begin with.

This ends the iteration. The next iteration re-evaluates all of the vertices and determines which is now the farthest off.

8.2.3   Contraction

Contraction occurs when the reflection point does not improve the rank of the worst point. Figure 8.6 shows the contraction scenario.

Figure 8.6: Contraction

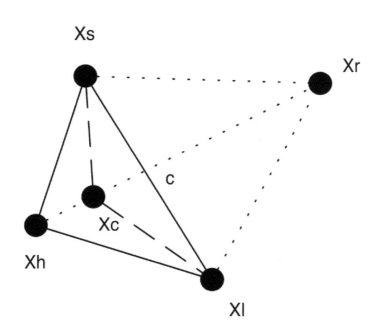

Continuing with the searcher analogy, the worst searcher at Xh had dreams of moving to Xr and getting a better rank. However, if the position at Xr had an even worse score, all we can do is move closer to the other two searchers. We still point toward the center of the two other searchers but, since our hopes have been dashed, we do not move beyond them. We move somewhere in the middle of the simplex, to location Xc. Hopefully this improves our rank.

Either way, the iteration is now done. The next iteration will rank the vertices again and continue.

8.3 Finishing the Nelder Mead Algorithm

It is important to know when to terminate an iterative algorithm such as Nelder Mead. This algorithm typically terminates based on the following three criteria.

- A maximum number of iterations is exceeded.

- The score is good enough.

- The vertices have become "close enough" to each other.

Once the algorithm completes, we consider the best vertex to be the solution. If the vertices have become close together, another option is to restart the algorithm by building a new simplex based on the best vertex. The search can then begin anew.

Nelder Mead is relatively efficient in that only one of the vertices needs to be reevaluated with each iteration. In machine learning, most computer processing time is spent evaluating against the training data. With Nelder Mead, it is only necessary to reevaluate one vertex because only the worst vertex moves.

In addition to reflection, contraction and expansion, some older implementations of Nelder Mead also made use of a shrink step. Later research found the shrink step to be unnecessary, however, and most modern implementations of Nelder Mead do not include it.

Unlike greedy random, simulated annealing and hill climbing, Nelder Mead performs a coordinated search from multiple locations at once. Such coordinated searches are very common in even more advanced algorithms. Particle Swarm Optimization (PSO) and Genetic Algorithms both use many multiple coordinated solutions.

8.4   Chapter Summary

This chapter introduced you to three optimization algorithms that can be used for training. These algorithms are designed to optimize individual values in a vector to obtain a better score for the model being trained. This vector is the long term memory for any of the machine learning algorithms we have seen so far.

Hill climbing is a simple search optimization algorithm. It starts at a vector location and evaluates moves that can be made from that vector. Whatever move results in the largest improvement to the score is taken. Hill climbing is very susceptible to local minima and maxima. Once hill climbing reaches a point where it can no longer find a better solution, the algorithm is complete.

Simulated annealing works somewhat like hill climbing, except that simulated annealing is sometimes willing to move to a position that has a lower score than the current position. Nelder Mead is another training algorithm that can be used to optimize a vector.

This chapter focused on continuous optimization algorithms. A continuous optimization algorithm deals primarily with floating point numbers. However, some optimization algorithms may be used on discrete data. The next chapter will demonstrate the optimization of discrete data.

Chapter 9

Discrete Optimization

- Discrete vs. Continuous

- The Knapsack Problem

- The Traveling Salesman Problem

In the last chapter, we saw that simulated annealing could be used to optimize the long-term memory of machine-learning algorithms. The optimization occurred against the long-term memory vector of a machine-learning algorithm. This vector was composed of continuous floating-point numbers. With continuous vectors, there is an infinite amount of additional numbers between two consecutive whole numbers. This is continuous data. Not all data is continuous.

This chapter will focus on using simulated annealing to analyze discrete problems, particularly focusing on the traveling salesman problem and the knapsack problem. The traveling salesman problem is discrete because it seeks to find the most optimal route to visit a fixed number of cities. The knapsack problem is discrete because it seeks to find an optimal set of items to put into a finite knapsack. Discrete data always deals with a finite number of items.

9.1　The Traveling Salesman Problem

Simulated annealing is commonly used to solve the traveling salesman problem (TSP), because the TSP is an NP-hard problem that generally cannot be solved by traditional iterative algorithms. TSP is one of most famous computer science problems. We will now see how to apply simulated annealing to it.

9.1.1　Understanding the Traveling Salesman Problem

The traveling salesman problem involves determining the shortest route for a "traveling salesman" who must visit a certain number of cities. The salesman is allowed to begin and end at any city, but must visit each city once and only once. There are several variants of the TSP, some of which allow multiple visitations to cities or assign different values to different cities. The TSP we will evaluate in this chapter simply seeks the shortest route to visit each city once. The TSP problem and shortest route used in this chapter are shown in Figure 9.1.

Figure 9.1: The Traveling Salesman

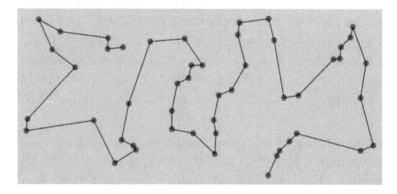

It may seem like finding the shortest route would be an easy task for a normal iterative program. However, as the number of cities increases, the number of possible combinations increases drastically. If there are one or two cities, only one route is possible. If there are three cities, the possible routes increase to six, however. The follow list shows how quickly the number of paths grow!

```
1 city has 1 path
2 cities have 1 path
3 cities have 6 paths
4 cities have 24 paths
5 cities have 120 paths
6 cities have 720 paths
7 cities have 5,040 paths
8 cities have 40,320 paths
9 cities have 362,880 paths
10 cities have 3,628,800 paths
11 cities have 39,916,800 paths
12 cities have 479,001,600 paths
13 cities have 6,227,020,800 paths
...
50 cities have 3.041 * 10^64 paths
```

The formula used to collect data for the above table is the factorial. The number of cities, n, is calculated using the factorial operator (!). The factorial of some arbitrary value n is given by n * (n - 1) * (n - 2) * ... * 3 * 2 * 1. These values become incredibly large when a program must do a "brute force" search. However, a simulated annealing algorithm such as the sample program examined in the next section finds the solution to a 50-city problem in a matter of minutes. (Behzad, 2002)

9.1.2 Implementing the Traveling Salesman Problem

So far, we have discussed the basic principles of continuous simulated annealing algorithms in previous chapters. The discrete version of simulated annealing is not too different from the continuous version that we saw in Chapter 8. The flow chart remains the same as what we saw in Figure 8.1. The difference is in how we move from the current position.

To conduct continuous simulated annealing, we would add a random value to one or more dimensions to move from the current position. In discrete simulated annealing, on the other hand, we need to be a little more creative. In the context of the TSP, each solution is a path through the cities. Our current position is this path. Moving to a new "position" means choosing a path similar to the current path.

It is important not to confuse the term "position" with city location. In this context, it does not refer to any particular "position" within the map of the cities. Rather, it describes one path among all possible paths to navigate that particular map. To move from one path to another, we simply flip the order of two cities in the original path. Flipping two cities ensures that we do not introduce a duplicate city.

To use simulated annealing, you must first generate an initial random solution. For TSP, this is a random list of the cities, with no duplicates. Then you must provide a means of creating a new solution through the implementation of a slight, randomized change For TSP, we simply flip the order in which the path visits two cities. This is implemented by choosing two random indexes (that are not the same) and exchanging their locations on the list.

There are three things that you must provide to any simulated annealing algorithm implementation.

- A scoring function to evaluate each position.

- A means of generating an initial random potential solution.

- A means of moving to a new random position based on your current position.

This is no different from continuous simulated annealing. The primary difference between the continuous and discrete annealing is in how these three aspects are implemented. For the traveling salesman problem, the score is simply the distance traveled, which is scored more highly as the distance travelled minimizes. The initial solution is the generation of a random, non-repeating list of cities. Movement to the new random position is implemented by flipping two cities.

9.2 Circular TSP

How can we evaluate an algorithms effectiveness with an NP-Hard problem? For an NP-Hard problem we often do not know the actual correct answer. This can make it very difficult to know exactly how close the algorithm has come to an optimal solution. There is a way to test the simulated annealing algorithm on a TSP, however. We can arrange the cities in a circle. If the cities are arranged in a circle, or oval, then the optimal path should run the perimeter of the shape. Figure 9.2 shows simulated annealing trying to optimize a path through cities arranged in an oval.

Figure 9.2: Annealing an Oval Path

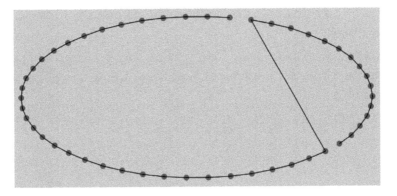

The annealing algorithm above came close to an optimal solution. However, it is not perfect. This is okay. You can rarely find a global optimum in any situation. It is only because we have insight into geometry that we can immediately spot that this path is not perfect. If you have insight into a problem that can help to solve it, then by all means, use it! AI is most useful when you have no other way to solve a problem.

9.3   The Knapsack Problem

The knapsack problem is a combinational optimization problem that has been
around as early as the late 1800s. The origin of the name is unknown, although
mathematician Tobias Dantzig suggested that the knapsack problem may have
originated as a folk story long before a formal mathematical problem was set
down.

9.3.1   Understanding the Knapsack Problem

The knapsack problem describes the dilemma of a burglar inside of a store.
He is surrounded by merchandise, but he only has one knapsack. What should
the burglar take to maximize his profit? The combination of items must fit
inside his knapsack.

In fact, anyone who has packed for a trip has faced a variant of the knapsack
problem. Figure 9.3 shows a knapsack and some items one might want for an
overnight camping trip.

Figure 9.3: The Knapsack Problem

The knapsack problem is a discrete problem. You can only select a fixed number of items and you are typically allowed to choose only zero or one of each item. This is the most common type of knapsack problem and it is called a 0-1 problem. Other variants allow for the selection of more than one of each individual item. The items are typically provided to the problem with weights and profit scores. You might wonder about volume in the knapsack problem. By convention, the knapsack problem does not consider volume. The maximum weight that will fit in the knapsack is also specified. (Pisinger, 2003)

9.3.2   Implementing the Knapsack Problem

Discrete simulated annealing can easily be applied to the knapsack problem. It is very important to think about how you might want to represent this problem. In the context of the knapsack problem, a solution is a list of items that does not exceed the weight limit imposed by the knapsack.

The best way to represent a potential knapsack solution is with a vector that has dimensions equal to the number of unique items that can be added to the knapsack. Each item's element in this vector will contain a whole number representing the count of that item taken. For example, Figure 9.3 describes the potential for bringing the following items.

```
Coffee thermos (weight=5, profit=1):  false
Baseball cap (weight=1, profit=1):  true
Blanket (weight=3, profit=10):  true
Bottle of water (weight=2, profit=25):  true
```

Out knapsack can hold a max weight of 7. The coffee thermos has been deemed unworthy, so that value is **false**. The rest has been determined to be profitable, so their values are **true**. The resulting weight is 6, which is below the maximum weight of 7. Adding the coffee would put us over the weight, while replacing anything else with the coffee would reduce our profit.

We now have a way to represent the solution. We must provide certain things to the simulated annealing algorithm.

- A scoring function to evaluate each position (set of items).

- A means of generating an initial random potential solution.

- A means of moving to a new random position based on the current position.

Simulated annealing always solves a minimization problem. This aspect must be considered during the creation of the scoring function. We would like to tie the maximum score to the profit generated by each item we take. The theoretical maximum profit is the sum of the profit of all items. If all the items fit in the knapsack, the theoretical maximum profit is attainable–otherwise, it is not.

We will use the difference between our current profit and the theoretical maximum as the best score. It is unlikely that we will ever get the optimal score of zero, which would indicate that every item can fit in the knapsack. If they can all fit, it hardly seems worthwhile to consider the problem. Rather, we instead attempt to approach perfection.

Another important feature to consider for the scoring function is what happens if the knapsack's maximum weight is exceeded in the solution. Ideally, our randomization would never let this happen. However, it does not hurt to check the maximum weight in the scoring function as well. If the knapsack's maximum weight is exceeded, then the score should be pushed out to a very large value. This will cause any invalid knapsack configuration to be discarded by the algorithm.

To meet the second provision to simulated annealing, we need a way to initialize a random solution. To initialize the first solution, start with an empty knapsack and add items to it one at a time. Once we add an item that exceeds the maximum weight of the knapsack, remove that item and consider the knapsack initialized.

To meet the third provision to simulated annealing, we need to generate a new position based on the current position. To randomize to a new state, add a new item that is not already in the knapsack. If this sets us over the maximum weight, choose a random item and remove it. Continue to remove items until the knapsack is below the maximum weight. The result will be the new position.

9.4   Chapter Summary

This chapter looked at how we might apply simulated annealing to a discrete problem. Discrete solutions are usually members of a finite set. For example, whole numbers in a range are discreet, as are colors.

There are very few differences between a continuous simulated annealing algorithm and a discrete one. Both require three components:

- A scoring function.

- A way to generate an initial random solution.

- A means of slightly changing a solution as we iterate through potential solutions.

The traveling salesman problem was introduced as a discrete problem. The traveling salesman seeks the shortest possible path through a number of cities. Brute force cannot be applied to this problem, as there are too many possibilities. Simulating annealing can be used to find an acceptable solution, however. The end result from simulated annealing may not be the global optimum, however, as finding the best solution is typically NP-Hard.

The knapsack problem is also discrete. This problem requires you to choose from a list of items that have varying weights and profit values to pack into a knapsack that can only hold so much weight. The goal is to maximize the profit for the weight our knapsack can hold.

The next chapter will conclude this book by introducing linear regression and general linear models. These are two very common statistical models that can be used with machine learning. Both linear regression and general linear models are valuable when used alone or as part of a larger algorithm.

Chapter 10

Linear Regression

- Linear Regression

- Generalized Linear Model (GLM)

- Link Function

This chapter will explore linear regression and generalized linear models (GLM). These are related statistical models that allow relationships to be established between input and output vectors. The input vector can contain multiple values, while the output vector must be a single value.

Linear regression allows for simple linear relationships to be modeled between the input and output vectors. These relationships can be used for some to learn basic problems, so long as the relationships are linear. Generalized linear models (GLM) add a link function to regular regression that greatly expands what can be modeled, as the relationship no longer needs to be linear. (Pedhazur, 1982)

10.1   Linear Regression

Linear regression attempts to map the input vector to the output vector with a relatively simple linear model. If you just have two variables, **x** and **y**, you can write a linear function from them. Equation 10.1 shows such an equation.

$$Y = mx + b \qquad (10.1)$$

Here **m** is the slope and **b** is the x-intercept. This function is called linear because on a graph it looks like a straight line. A curve in the line would indicate that the function is not linear.

The following equation gives values to the unknowns in Equation 10.1.

$$Y = 0.5x + 2 \qquad (10.2)$$

The slope is 0.5 and the x-intercept is 2. Figure 10.1 shows the graph of this equation.

Figure 10.1: Graph of Y = 0.5x + 2

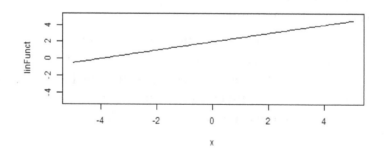

Equation 10.1 is a simple, single variable linear regression model. A linear regression dealing with only a single variable is called univariate. A very common example used to demonstrate univariate regressions is the relationship of shoe size to a person's height. This regression would accept a single input of the person's height and output their shoe size, or vice versa. Training such

a model would involve finding the slope and y-intercept that describes the relationship between height and shoe size.

The above graph shows that the function is linear. The function has a positive slope, which is evident in the line's northeast to southwest orientation. The slope is also only 0.5, so the line is not greatly inclined. Because the y-intercept is 2, we know that when x is zero, y will be 2.

Many problems consist of several inputs, however. Such models are called multivariate. A multivariate linear regression looks very similar to a univariate. The only difference is that you have one term for each of the inputs. Additionally, you still have the y-intercept. Equation 10.2 shows the general form of a multivariate linear regression.

$$y_i = \beta_1 x_{i1} + \cdots + \beta_p x_{ip} + \varepsilon_i = \mathbf{x}_i^{\mathrm{T}} \boldsymbol{\beta} + \varepsilon_i, \qquad i = 1, \ldots, n \qquad (10.3)$$

In the above equation, the **x** variables represent the input vector. There will be a total of **n** inputs. You should notice that each of the inputs is multiplied by a corresponding beta value. Finally, an epsilon value is added. Epsilon represents the y-intercept. Despite all the additional terms, the above equation is still linear. Any such model would produce a straight line graph.

We will focus on the multivariate linear regression. Univariate linear regression is really just a special case of multivariate regression. Thus, it is not worth learning to do two separate algorithms.

The beta and epsilon values are coefficients. Even epsilon is a coefficient of one. These coefficients make up the long-term memory for this model. We could use any of the learning algorithms presented in this book to find decent coefficients that produce the desired outputs from the inputs in your training set.

10.1.1   Least Squares Fitting

Training is the process of determining what coefficients will most closely match your training set. Once you have your coefficients, it is easy to calculate the output of a linear regression. It is unlikely that coefficients will be fit enough to allow the model to represent every training case. However, training will attempt to minimize the overall error of your training set elements.

Most documentation on linear regression uses the word "fitting"to describe the process of training. Both terms really mean the same thing. As stated in the previous section, you could use any of the training algorithms in this book to fit proper coefficients to the model. The training algorithms presented so far are all general-purpose algorithms. They do not specify any requirements on the long-term memory (in this case, coefficients) that they are trying to fit. We will now see a training algorithm designed specifically for linear regression.

Often, mathematical solutions will produce a better solution faster than general algorithms. If you do not know of an appropriate mathematical solution, then by all means use a general algorithm. The only real downside is that the training time will likely be longer. I've occasionally implemented a general solution only to have a more mathematically advanced friend say, "Oh interesting, you decided not to go with the [insert advanced mathematical technique here] approach." Though, I am always quite glad to have such shortcuts shown to me. Math is an infinite loop of learning.

Now we will look at one such mathematical solution in order to use least squares fitting. This training algorithm will not work on any of the previous models or machine learning algorithms presented in this book. The only algorithm in this book with which you can use least squares fitting is linear regression, as least square fitting is not a general-purpose algorithm.

To fit using least squares, we must create two matrixes. These matrixes will be named **matrixX** and **matrixY**. Both matrixes will have a number of rows equal to the number of training set elements. The matrix **matrixX** will hold all of the inputs from the training set. Thus, it will have a number of columns equal to the input count plus 1. Each input in the matrix should have a one concatenated to it. This allows the y-intercept to be accounted for. The matrix **matrixY** will hold all of the ideal outputs from the training set. For linear regression, there should be only one output, so the column count for **matrixY** will always be 1.

Using these two matrixes, we can get a good fit of coefficients for the linear regression. We will use a linear algebra technique called matrix decomposition, of which there are many different kinds. Matrix decomposition is essentially a factorization. Factoring the matrix separates the matrix into two matrixes that, when multiplied together, produce the original matrix.

For sum of squares, we will not use the two factor matrixes, but rather use the QR decomposition to solve this system of equations. QR decomposition is commonly used in AI. It is the main component of the least squares training algorithm. (Barlow, 1993)

10.1.2 Least Squares Fitting Example

Let's create a linear regression model that will convert Fahrenheit temperatures into Celsius using least squares fitting. We will begin with some training data.

```
0 -> 32
100 -> 212
```

The above data simply states that 0 degrees Celsius is equal to 32 degrees Fahrenheit. Likewise, 100 degrees Celsius is 212 degrees Fahrenheit. We would like to calculate the slope and y-intercept for a linear equation that will produce the desired output shown above.

We must generate the **matrixX** and **matrixY** matrixes. First, we generate **matrixX**. As previously stated, this is essentially the input values with a 1 concatenated. The 1 represents the y-intercept. **matrixX** is described below.

```
[0.0 ,1.0]
[100.0 ,1.0]
```

Next, we construct **matrixY**, which is a matrix of ideal outputs.

```
[32.0]
[212.0]
```

The next step is to solve the matrix, using QR decomposition, and obtain the coefficients. I am not going to show you the internals of a QR decomposition, as this is a "wheel" I've never tried to reinvent. I always use a linear algebra package to perform this operation. There are quite a few linear algebra packages to choose from in most programming languages. Some are very efficient. You might choose to use a natively implemented linear algebra package or GPU based linear algebra package. BLAS is a very common linear algebra package, and there is a version of BLAS for CUDA GPUs called CUBLAS. GPUs can often perform matrix operations considerably faster than CPUs.

We will solve **matrixX** for **matrixY** using QR. This will return the coefficients that must be applied to **matrixX** to produce **matrixY**. We will only get one set of coefficients, despite the fact that we have two rows. These coefficients will produce the best results possible over all rows. This results in the following matrix:

```
[1.8]
[32.0]
```

The matrix describes a coefficient and the y-intercept. The y-intercept is always given by the one that we concatenated to every input. As previously stated, the y-intercept has a coefficient of 1. Therefore, the following linear model can be used to convert Celsius to Fahrenheit:

```
f = (c*1.8)+32
```

This matches the conversion formulas found in Wikipedia and other sources.

There are no iterations with the least squares fit. It is not necessary to perform multiple iterations of least squares fitting, unlike other iteration-based algorithms seen in previous chapters.

10.1.3   Anscombe's Quartet

Linear regression requires that the relationship between inputs and outputs be linear, but it can be problematic to force a line from data points. Anscombe's Quartet is a special data set that points out some issues in linear regression. Figure 10.2 shows Anscombe's Quartet. (Anscombe, 1973)

Figure 10.2: Anscombe's Quartet

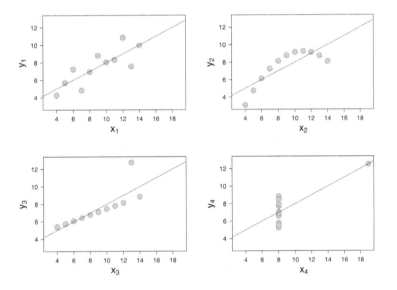

The above figure shows four different data sets. The points in each of these four look clearly different. All four of these produce the exact same linear regression coefficients. The line drawn through the points represents the linear regression. That these four all produce the same linear regression indicates some of the flaws in the system.

The top-left plot shows a linear regression line that does a pretty good job approximating the relationship between the points. However, the top-right data set is not at all linear. The bottom two show the effect that outliers can have on a model. An outlier occurs when a small number of points are completely out of sequence with the others.

10.1.4 Abalone Data Set

An example is provided for fitting a linear regression to the Abalone Data Set, which contains observations of abalone sea snails. The data set can be obtained from the following URL.

http://archive.ics.uci.edu/ml/datasets/Abalone

The set fits a linear regression to predict the number of rings in the abalone using a number of other observations. Much like a tree, the ring count of an abalone indicates its age. The output from this set is as follows. (Nash, 1994)

```
[0.0, 1.0, 0.0, 0.455, 0.365, 0.095, 0.514, 0.2245, 0.101, 0.15]
    -> [9.1279296875], Ideal: [15.0]
[0.0, 1.0, 0.0, 0.35, 0.265, 0.09, 0.2255, 0.0995, 0.0485, 0.07]
    -> [7.75634765625], Ideal: [7.0]
[1.0, 0.0, 0.0, 0.53, 0.42, 0.135, 0.677, 0.2565, 0.1415, 0.21] ->
    [11.078125], Ideal: [9.0]
[0.0, 1.0, 0.0, 0.44, 0.365, 0.125, 0.516, 0.2155, 0.114, 0.155]
    -> [9.5615234375], Ideal: [10.0]
[0.0, 0.0, 1.0, 0.33, 0.255, 0.08, 0.205, 0.0895, 0.0395, 0.055]
    -> [6.69970703125], Ideal: [7.0]
[0.0, 0.0, 1.0, 0.425, 0.3, 0.095, 0.3515, 0.141, 0.0775, 0.12] ->
    [7.7802734375], Ideal: [8.0]
[1.0, 0.0, 0.0, 0.53, 0.415, 0.15, 0.7775, 0.237, 0.1415, 0.33] ->
    [13.52197265625], Ideal: [20.0]
```

It provides the ring count predicted for each abalone, as well as the ideal ring count according to the training data.

10.2 Generalized Linear Models

Generalized linear models (GLM) are based on the linear regression models discussed above. They make use of a link function to further abstract the output from the GLM. There are a variety of link functions that can be used with GLMs. Because GLMs are trained with a calculus-based training algorithm, the link function must have a derivative. The use of derivatives for GLM training will be described in the next section.

The equation for a GLM is very similar to that for linear regression. The primary difference is that a GLM adds a link function.

The equation for a GLM is shown in Equation 10.3.

$$y_i = g(\beta_1 x_{i1} + \cdots + \beta_p x_{ip} + \varepsilon_i = \mathbf{x}_i^{\mathrm{T}} \boldsymbol{\beta} + \varepsilon_i), \qquad i = 1, \ldots, n \qquad (10.4)$$

You may have noticed that Equation 10.3 is very similar to Equation 10.2. This is because the GLM is essentially the return value of a linear regression passed to the link function. In the above equation, the link function is given by $\mathbf{g}()$. The input vector is $\mathbf{x}$, while the output is $\mathbf{y}$. The beta values make up the coefficients and the epsilon value is the y-intercept, which is the same as with linear regression. The only addition is the link function.

There are many different link functions to choose from. One of the most common is the logistic, or logit, function. A GLM that uses the logit function is typically called a logistic regression model. The output of a logistic regression is always considered to be one of two values.

If you would like to model something with two categories, then you should consider using a logistic regression model. Logistic regression chooses between two options based on the input. This might be true/false, good/bad, buy/sell, etc. If you need to choose between more than two options, you could use the RBF networks presented in this book.

The logit function is sometimes called a sigmoid function. It is shown in Figure 10.3.

Figure 10.3: The Logistic Function

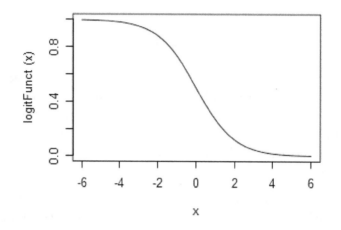

The logistic function is able to scale the output from the linear regression. It has several very important properties:

- g(-Infinity) = 0

- g(Infinity) = 1

- g(0) = 1/2

- g(-x) = 1 - g(x)

- if x > y then g(x) > g(y)

The output of the logit will never be less than zero or more than one. Therefore, 0 is typically mapped to one of the categories that the GLM aims to predict, while 1 is mapped to the other category. A value of 0 results in a half, which is exactly between 0 and 1.

The sigmoid function is also monotonic. Monotonic refers to the fact that the function is either consistently increasing or decreasing. Monotonic functions do not reverse that direction.

10.2.1   Reweight Least Squares Training

GLMs can be trained using any of the general training algorithms presented in this book. However, there is a mathematical shortcut in the form of the reweight least squares training algorithm. This training algorithm is based on the least squares training, but reweight least squares training can handle the addition of the link function. Unlike least squares, the reweight least squares algorithm is iterative. You will need to process iterations until the error is acceptable. (Chartrand, 2008)

The reweight least squares algorithm falls into a category of training algorithms called gradient descent. The back propagation-training algorithm also falls under the category of gradient descent; you might be familiar with back propagation training if you've ever worked with neural networks.

Gradient descent makes use of calculus to determine the gradient of the error function at the current state of the long-term memory (the coefficients). This gradient will indicate whether we need to increase or decrease each coefficient to lower the error. To do this, we need to determine the derivative of the link function, which means that link functions must be differentiable (have a derivative) in order to perform gradient descent.

The derivative of a function is just another function. The derivative function tells us the instantaneous rate of change for the first function. Consider a function that describes the position of a car at any given time. If you pass the value 10 seconds into the function, it tells you the position of the car at 10 seconds. Likewise, if you pass in 60 seconds, you will be given the position of the car at that time. If you were to take the derivative of the function describing position at time, you would have a new function that describes the speed of the car at any time.

When plotted on a graph, the derivative usually looks like a line that touches the main function at only one point. Consider whether Figure 10.4 represents the error as you varied only one coefficient.

Figure 10.4: Error Derivative from Varying Single Coefficient

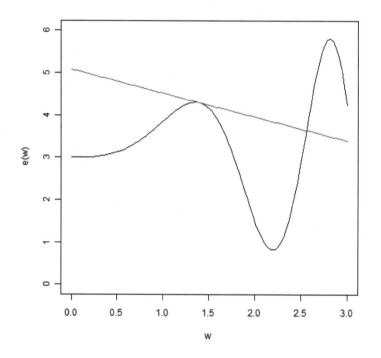

The curvy line shows the error function **e**() as you vary the coefficient **w**. The straight line is the derivative of the error function at a given **w**. Notice how the slope of the derivative tells us the direction in which the underlying function is heading. The goal is to descend to the lowest point, which is somewhere between 2.0 and 2.5. The point at which it touches is currently at 1.5 (the location of the derivative). Therefore, by the slope (or gradient) of the derivative, we must increase **w**. This is called gradient descent, because we use the gradients to descend.

During training, the program cannot visualize this graph. All that we can see is one narrow vertical slice, in which exist the error at our current coefficient value and the derivative. We move the coefficient in the direction indicated by the derivative and see how much the error improves in the next iteration. In the next iteration, we calculate a new gradient and continue to adjust the coefficient. This same process continues until we can no longer improve the error by a considerable amount.

10.3 Chapter Summary

This chapter introduced two forms of linear regression: regular linear regression and generalized linear models. Regular linear regression requires that a mostly linear relationship exist between the input vector and output values. Linear regression outputs a single resulting value.

A linear regression algorithm's long-term memory is the coefficients that are used by its equation. These coefficients can be adjusted using the general training algorithms used earlier in this book. However, there a mathematical shortcut that can be employed to quickly determine values for the coefficients that minimize the error between the output from the model and the expected outputs contained in the training set.

You will see several such shortcuts through this series. There are general algorithms that can be used to solve nearly any type of problem, and there are specialized algorithms that only work with specific models. The special algorithms often use mathematical techniques to perform very efficient optimization of the underlying models. Least squares training and reweight least squares training are two such examples.

This book introduced you to many fundamental algorithms for AI. Subsequent volumes in this series will build more complex algorithms that make use of the fundamental algorithms in this book. While these algorithms are often used as building blocks, they are also very useful in their own right.

The next book in this series will cover nature inspired algorithms. The only model that we have for true intelligence is the human brain and nature. Because of this, it is natural that we take inspiration from nature to design algorithms. Genetic algorithms, genetic programming, ant colony optimization, particle swarm optimization, and other such algorithms will be explored in the next book. The next book uses many of the algorithms introduced in this book.

Appendix A

Examples

- Downloading Examples

- Structure of Example Download

- Keeping Updated

A.1 Artificial Intelligence for Humans

These examples are part of a series of books that is currently under development. Check the above website to see which volumes have been completed and are available. The planned list is shown here.

The following volumes are planned for this series:

- Volume 0: Introduction to the Math of AI

- Volume 1: Fundamental Algorithms

- Volume 2: Nature Inspired Algorithms

- Volume 3: Neural Networks

- Volume 4: Support Vector Machines

- Volume 5: Probabilistic Learning

A.2   Staying Up to Date

This appendix describes how to obtain the "Artificial Intelligence for Humans" (AIFH) book series examples.

This is probably the most dynamic area of the book. Computer languages are always changing and adding new versions. I will update the examples as this becomes necessary. There are also bugs and corrections. You are encouraged to always make sure you are using the latest version of the book examples.

Because this area is so dynamic, this file may have become out of date. You can always find the latest version of this file at the following location.

https://github.com/jeffheaton/aifh

A.3   Obtaining the Examples

This book's examples are provided in a number of computer programming languages. Core example packs are provided for Java, C#, C/C++, Python and R for most volumes. The community may have added other languages as well. All examples can be found at the GitHub repository.

https://github.com/jeffheaton/aifh

You have your choice of two different ways to download the examples.

A.3.1   Download ZIP File

Github provides an icon that allows you to simply download a ZIP file that contains all of the example code for the series. A single ZIP file is used to contain all of the examples for the series. Because of this, the contents of this ZIP are frequently updated. If you are starting a new volume, it is very important that you make sure you have the latest copy. The download can be performed from the following URL.

https://github.com/jeffheaton/aifh

You can see the download link in Figure A.1.

Figure A.1: GitHub

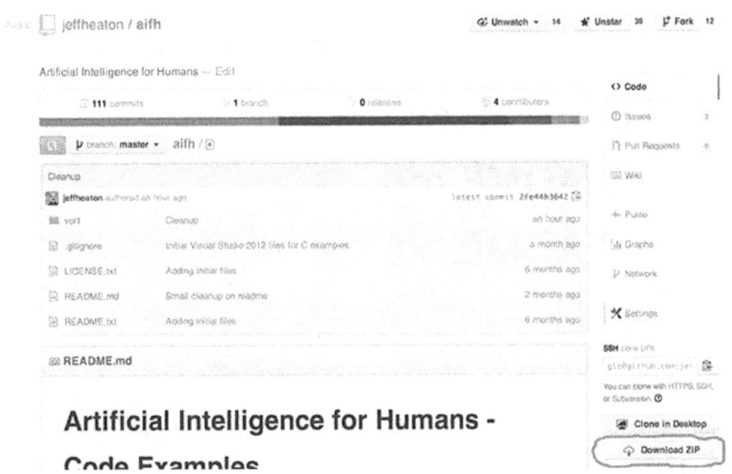

A.3.2   Clone the Git Repository

All examples can be obtained using the source control program **git**, if it is installed on your system. The following command clones the examples to your computer. Cloning simply refers to the process of copying the example files.

```
git clone https://github.com/jeffheaton/aifh.git
```

You can also pull the latest updates using the following command.

```
git pull
```

If you would like an introduction to **git** refer to the following URL.

http://git-scm.com/docs/gittutorial

A.4   Example Contents

The entire "Artificial Intelligence for Humans" series is contained in one download. This download is a zip file.

Once you open the examples file you will see the contents see in Figure A.2.

Figure A.2: Examples Download

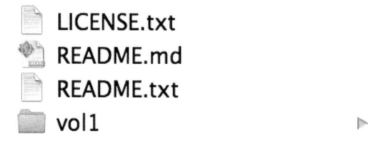

The license file describes the license used for the book examples. All of the examples for this series are released under the Apache v2.0 license. This is a Free and open-source software (FOSS) license. This means that I do retain a copyright to the files. However, you can freely reuse these files in both commercial and non-commercial projects without further permission.

While the book source code is provided free, the book text is not provided free. These books are commercial products that I sell through a variety of means. You may not redistribute the actual books. This includes the PDF, MOBI, EPUB and any other format the book might be converted to. I do, however, provide all books in DRM-free form. Your support of this policy is greatly appreciated and does contribute to the future growth of these books.

There are also two README files included in the download. The README.md is a "markdown" file that contains images and formatting. The README.txt file is plain text. Both files contain the same information. For more information on MD files, refer to the following URL.

https://help.github.com/articles/github-flavored-markdown

You will find README files at several levels of the examples download. The README file contained in the examples root (seen above) contains information about the book series.

You will also notice the individual volume folders contained in the download. These are named vol1, vol2, etc. You may not see all of the volumes in the download. Not all of the volumes have been written yet! All of the volumes have the same format. For example, if you were to open Volume 1, you would see the contents listed in Figure A.3.

Figure A.3: Inside Volume 1

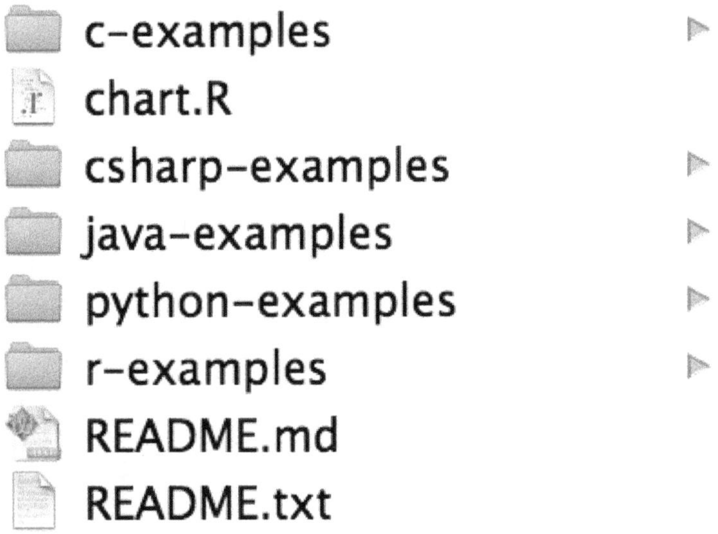

c-examples

chart.R

csharp-examples

java-examples

python-examples

r-examples

README.md

README.txt

Again, you see the two README files. These files contain information unique to this particular volume. The most important information contained in the volume level README files is the current status of the examples. The community often contributes example packs. This means that some of the example packs may not be complete. The README for the volume will let you know this important information. The volume README.also contains the errata and FAQ for a volume.

You should also see a file named "chart.R". This file contains the source code that I used to create many of the charts in the book. I use the R programming language to produce nearly all graphs and charts seen in the book. This allows you to see the equations behind the pictures. I do not translate this file to other programming languages. R is simply what I use in the production of the book. If I used another language, like Python, to produce some of the charts, you would see a "chart.py" along with the R code.

You can see that the above volume contains examples for C, C#, Java, Python and R. These are the core languages that I try to always ensure complete examples for. However, you may see other languages added. Again, always check the README file for the latest information on language translations.

Figure A.4 shows the contents of a typical language pack.

Figure A.4: The Java Language Pack

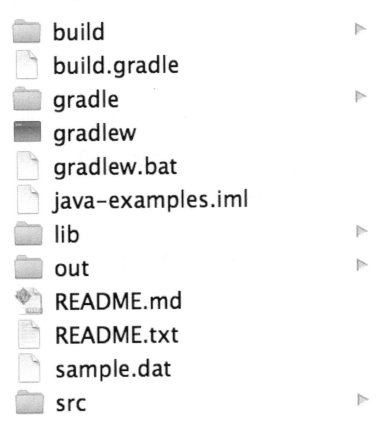

Notice the README files again? The README files inside of a language folder are VERY important. Inside the above two README files you will find information about using the examples with Java. If you are having trouble using the book's examples with a particular language, the README file should be your first stop. The other files seen above are all unique to Java. The README file above describes these in much greater detail.

A.5   Contributing to the Project

Do you want to translate the examples to a new language? Have you found something broken, misspelled, or otherwise botched? You probably have. Fork the project and push a commit revision to GitHub. You will be credited among the growing number of contributors.

The process begins with a fork. You create an account on GitHub and fork the AIFH project. This creates a new project, with a copy of the AIFH files. You will then clone your new for, in a similar way as was described for cloning the main AIFH repositiory. Once you make your changes you submit a "pull request". Once I get this request I will evaluate your changes/additions and merge it with the main project.

A much more detailed article on contributing through GitHub can be found here.

https://help.github.com/articles/fork-a-repo

References

This section lists the reference materials for this book.

Anscombe, F. J. (1973). "Graphs in Statistical Analysis". *American Statistician*

Bäck, Thomas, Evolutionary Algorithms in Theory and Practice (1996), p. 120, *Oxford Univ. Press*

Banzhaf, Wolfgang; Nordin, Peter; Keller, Robert; Francone, Frank (1998). *Genetic Programming - An Introduction*. San Francisco, CA: Morgan Kaufmann.

Barlow, Jesse L. (1993). "Chapter 9: Numerical aspects of Solving Linear Least Squares Problems". In Rao, *C.R. Computational Statistics. Handbook of Statistics 9*. North-Holland. ISBN 0-444-88096-8

Behzad, Arash; Modarres, Mohammad (2002), "New Efficient Transformation of the Generalized Traveling Salesman Problem into Traveling Salesman Problem"

Bishop, Christopher M. (1996) Neural Networks for Pattern Recognition. Oxford University Press

Bostrom, Nick "Are You Living In a Computer Simulation?" *Philosophical Quarterly*, 2003, Vol. 53, No. 211, pp. 243-255.

Box, G. E. P. and Mervin E. Muller, A Note on the Generation of Random Normal Deviates, *The Annals of Mathematical Statistics* (1958), Vol. 29, No. 2 pp. 610-611

Chartrand, R.; Yin, W. (March 31 - April 4, 2008). "Iteratively reweighted algorithms for compressive sensing". *IEEE International Conference on Acoustics, Speech and Signal Processing (ICASSP)*, 2008. pp. 3869-3872.

Das, A. & Chakrabarti, B. K. (2005). Quantum Annealing and Related Optimization Methods, Lecture Note in Physics, Vol. 679, *Springer, Heidelberg*

Deza, Elena & Deza, Michel Marie Deza (2009) Encyclopedia of Distances, page 94, *Springer.*

Draper, N.R.; Smith, H. (1998). Applied Regression Analysis (3rd ed.). *John Wiley.* ISBN 0-471-17082-8.

Fisher,R.A. "The use of multiple measurements in taxonomic problems" *Annual Eugenics*, 7, Part II, 179-188 (1936)

Green, Colin (2009). "Speciation by k-means Clustering". https://sites.google.com/site/sharpneat/speciation/speciation-by-k-means-clustering

Guiver, John P., and Klimasauskas, Casimir, C. (1991). "Applying Neural Networks, Part IV: Improving Performance." *PC AI*, July/August

Hamerly, G. and Elkan, C. (2002). "Alternatives to the k-means algorithm that find better clusterings". *Proceedings of the eleventh international conference on Information and knowledge management (CIKM).*

Harris, Zellig (1954). "Distributional Structure". *Word 10* (2/3): 146-62.

Koch, Christof (2013). "Decoding 'the Most Complex Object in the Universe" *Science Friday*, June 14, 2013.

Krause, Eugene F (Apr 2, 2012). Taxicab Geometry: An Adventure in Non-Euclidean Geometry, *Dover Books on Mathematics*

Lial, Margaret, Hornsby, John, Schneider, David I., Daniels, Callie. (2010) College Algebra (11th Edition). *Pearson.*

Lyons, Richard G. (November 2010) Understanding Digital Signal Processing (3rd Edition). *Prentice Hall*

Masters, T. (1993). Practical Neural Network Recipes in C++. New York: *Academic Press.*

Matsumoto, M.; Nishimura, T. (1998). "Mersenne twister: a 623-dimensionally equidistributed uniform pseudo-random number generator". *ACM Transactions on Modeling and Computer Simulation*

Marsaglia, G.; Zaman, A. (1991). "A new class of random number generators". *Annals of Applied Probability 1* (3): 462-480.

Nash, Warwick J, Sellers, Tracy L., Talbot, Simon R, Cawthorn, Andrew J. & Ford, Wes B. (1994) "The Population Biology of Abalone in Tasmania. I. Blacklip Abalone (_H. rubra_) from the North Coast and Islands of Bass Strait", *Sea Fisheries Division, Technical Report No. 48* (ISSN 1034-3288)

Nelder, John A.; R. Mead (1965). "A simplex method for function minimization". *Computer Journal* 7: 308-313.

Pedhazur, Elazar J (1982). Multiple regression in behavioral research: Explanation and prediction (2nd ed.). New York: *Holt, Rinehart and Winston.* ISBN 0-03-041760-0

Pisinger, D. 2003. Where are the hard knapsack problems? Technical Report 2003/08, *Department of Computer Science, University of Copenhagen, Copenhagen, Denmark.*

Quinlan,R. (1993). Combining Instance-Based and Model-Based Learning. In Proceedings on the Tenth International Conference of Machine Learning, 236-243, University of Massachusetts, Amherst. *Morgan Kaufmann.*

Robert, Christian & Casella, George (August, 2005). Monte Carlo Statistical Method. *Springer Texts in Statistics*

Ross, Sheldon (2002). A First Course in Probability, pp. 279-81

Russell, Stuart & Norvig, Peter (2009). Artificial Intelligence: A Modern Approach (3rd Edition). *Prentice Hall*

Siegel, George J., Hines, Edward Jr., Agranoff, Bernard W., Fisher, Stephen K. (1999) "Basic Neurochemistry: Molecular, Cellular and Medical Aspects Sixth Edition" ISBN 0-397-51820-X

Turing, Alan 1948, "Intelligent Machinery." Reprinted in "Cybernetics: Key Papers." Ed. C.R. Evans and A.D.J. Robertson. Baltimore: *University Park Press*, 1968. p. 31.

Index

CPSIA information can be obtained
at www.ICGtesting.com
Printed in the USA
LVHW022105070623
749042LV00012B/189

9 781493 682225